FLAMES FROM THE UNCONSCIOUS

FLAMES FROM THE UNCONSCIOUS

Trauma, Madness, and Faith

Michael Eigen

KARNAC

First published in 2009 by
Karnac Books Ltd
118 Finchley Road, London NW3 5HT

British Library Cataloguing in Publication Data

A C.I.P. for this book is available from the British Library

ISBN-13: 978 1 85575 699 1

Edited, designed and produced by The Studio Publishing Services Ltd,
www.publishingservicesuk.co.uk
e-mail: studio@publishingservicesuk.co.uk

www.karnacbooks.com

CONTENTS

To all who helped me

ACKNOWLEDGEMENTS

Chapter Two: "Primary aloneness" first appeared in 2008 in *Psychoanalytic Perspectives*, 5(2).

Chapter Three: "Incommunicado core and boundless supporting unknown" was originally published in 2007 in the *European Journal of Psychotherapy, Counselling & Research*, 9(4): 415–422. It is used here with permission of the journal and Taylor & Francis.

Chapter Four: "Guilt in an age of psychopathy" was originally published in 2007 in *The Psychoanalytic Review*, 94(5). It is used with permission of the National Psychological Association for Psychoanalysis. This paper is also part of a book, *Age of Psychopathy*, online at the Human Nature site (http://www.psychoanalysis-and-therapy. com/human_nature/eigen/pref.html), published in Italian, *Eta Di Psicopatia* (FrancoAngelli, 2007).

Chapter Five: "I killed Socrates" grew out of a panel, "What is Guilt?" at the Philoctetes Society (February, 2007) and a version of it is on the Society's website at: http://www.philoctetes.org/documents/ I%20Killed%20Socrates.pdf.

Chapter Six: An earlier version of "Revenge ethics" was published in 2005 in *Voices: The Art and Science of Psychotherapy*, 41: 73–76. It is used with permission of the journal and the American Academy of Psychotherapists (aapweb.com).

Chapter Nine: A shorter version of "Faith and destructiveness" was in a newsletter of the Institute for Psychotherapy Training 2006–2007, Volume 5 (www.nyipt.org/NYIPT%20Today%202006.pdf). It also appeared on dharmacafe.com (www.dharmacafe.com/index.php/life-cycles/article/faith-and-disillusionment-an-interview-with-dr-michael-eigen/). It is used here with permission of Regina Monte and the Institute for Psychotherapy Training.

Appendix: "Something wrong: Grace" is a dramatic monologue abstracted from Chapter Seven. In this monologue, Grace is the only speaker. It was written for the online magazine, *Moondance* Summer, 2006, published by the Women Artists and Writers International (http://www.moondance.org/2006/summer2006/fiction/wrong.html). Martha Frisoli Gibson supplied the stage directions.

ABOUT THE AUTHOR

Michael Eigen, PhD, has been deeply engaged in the depth psychologies for over fifty years. He began writing papers for professional journals in the 1970s and since 1986 has published seventeen books. Currently, he is on the faculty of the National Psychological Association for Psychoanalysis and the New York University Postdoctoral Program in Psychotherapy and Psychoanalysis. He has given a weekly seminar on Bion, Winnicott, and Lacan for over thirty-five years. His work is dedicated to exploring psychic reality and interweaves with spiritual and social dimensions of daily life.

Books by Michael Eigen

Karnac publications

The Psychotic Core (1986, 2004)
The Electrified Tightrope (Ed. Adam Phillips) (1993, 2004)
Psychic Deadness (1996, 2004)
Toxic Nourishment (1999)
Damaged Bonds (2001)
Feeling Matters (2007)
Conversations with Michael Eigen (with Aner Govrin) (2008)

Other publications

Coming Through the Whirlwind (1992)
Reshaping the Self (1995)
The Psychoanalytic Mystic (1998)
Ecstasy (2001)
Rage (2002)
The Sensitive Self (2004)
Emotional Storm (2005)
Lust (2006)
Age of Psychopathy (2007)

"set free and alive for goodness"
Kjell von Krogh

"The principles of psychical growth are not known"
W. R. Bion

"Meditation—unknown intimacies"
Michael Eigen

CHAPTER ONE

Introduction

I s *flames* too strong a word? I want to connote fire, intensity, burning, inspiration. Our culture long associated flames with hell. Quite scary: to burn in hell forever for your sins, for the evil in you, for the evil you did. Fire, also, was associated with creativity, creative heat, in-flammation, a flame within. Poets tend to gravitate towards the latter, inner flame. For William Blake, the Devil, as well as Jesus, is important for fecundity of creative imagination. We can speak of hells of creative passion, creative work, self-creation, and discovery.

Fires of the mind, the gut, the passions, holy and hellish fires, eternal flames. I heard a great rabbi speak of "the fire that never goes out" and read saints who speak of burning away the dross of self, burning away self itself. Fire associated with purity as well as sin. The same rabbi, Menachem Schneerson, who spoke of the eternal flame within, also spoke of self-nullification. As if burning away the self lays bare the eternal flame.

I will not recount all usages of flame: fires of disaster, cooking, warmth of hearth and home, love and hate fires of all sorts, fearsome, majestic flames of nature, and our great venture to control the uncontrollable, what we gain, lose, unleash. One more will do for my purpose: theft, the Greek myth of Prometheus, who steals fire from the gods as a gift to humanity. A civilizing gift that spans physical, emotional, and mental levels. A gift that requires cultivation and growth of ability to channel dangerous energy.

Is there an Ur word or image in which all these and other meanings of fire meld? A root sign or symbol from which a spectrum of meanings develops? A compressed density that unfolds and proliferates over time with usage? The commingling of theft with gift seems of particular importance to personality, uniting fires of sin and discovery.

To feel like an impostor is a recurrent theme among artists, and to feel false as a person is a crucial theme in psychoanalysis. The sense that one is living a lie is important to many and often goes with a sense that an important flame is waning. Fused with this is fear that self-discovery is sinful. Guilt, fear, and shame attaches to development *and* to failure to develop. Fusion of opposites is the rule in psychic life. Creative theft melds with destructive dreads. Unbearable agonies prompt easeful lies and falsity to escape pain and helplessness.

Falsity is part of growing up (part of the reason Holden Caulfield in *The Catcher in the Rye* sees adults as phoney). Threads of truth remain. One longs for their development and may seek to grow in capacity to connect with and mediate them. We are all midwives to ourselves. We fear if we are too much ourselves we will destroy ourselves, but failing in this task also involves self-injury.

It may sound odd to some to hear me speak of D. W. Winnicott as a flame from the unconscious. So much of his writing seems gentle, and no other psychoanalyst goes as far as he in validating the importance of quietude. He gives expression to dialectics between quiet and excited states, the positive contributions of each. So often, quiet states get shorted. Not by Winnicott. He feels they have much to offer, gentle flames.

The fact that he so values quiet is brought home even more because he values extreme states as well. Extremes make aliveness more colourful. So much so, he created a prayer, something like, "Lord, may I be alive when I die." He did not want to miss out on aliveness, not even (especially?) the aliveness of death. How alive can one be when one dies? Winnicott would give it his best shot to experience something as important as dying.

I do not remember flames being a big part of Winnicott's language, but he spoke of "sparks". Particularly, a *vital spark* each of us possesses, or is, or can be, a spark of aliveness that has a biography. Our vital spark undergoes vicissitudes, hardships, trauma, and also facilitating threads, support, and nourishment of many kinds. The events of life interact with our aliveness in ways that aid and hinder it and, at times, the light can grow dim indeed, for periods gone. In latter instances, therapy is like lighting matches near the mouth of a corpse, looking for signs of life, fanning sparks where embers seemed out.

My emphasis in the next two chapters is the aliveness Winnicott finds in aloneness, and the contribution aloneness makes to aliveness. The alone self gets a bad rap in our culture, where phoney outgoingness is emphasized. There is something wrong with you if you are alone. You are withdrawn, in some way disabled, missing out on real living done by everyone else.

This negative evaluation of aloneness carries over into devaluing an alone aspect of self that is with us all our lives. Winnicott adds a subtle turn to experiencing aloneness. He envisions an aloneness that is made possible by support the alone one does not know s/he has, e.g., the support an infant gets without being able to cognize it. Winnicott posits an important sense of aloneness, perhaps from the beginning of life, a precious sense that is traumatized by lack of support. Good quality aloneness depends on good quality support. Failure to support the infant's alone self results in deformations in the sense of self. Deformations are inevitable. No one evades trauma. A certain balance is important. Much depends on the quality of support an infant does not know it has. If the balance tips overly towards too little support, or too much of the wrong kind (invasive, engulfing), self-feeling becomes skewed and taints the way life "feels" develop.

Chapters Two ("Primary aloneness") and Three ("Incommunicado core and boundless supporting unknown") explore aspects of Winnicott's alone self in his writings, with my patients, and in my own life. How the self feels in infancy becomes part of a background atmosphere influencing the feel of life as it unfolds. Skews, once established, play a role in the taste of things and slant experiences that come one's way. Winnicott speaks of early parental environment, but the spirit of the time, the tone of society, has an impact. The goodness/badness of the world around the parents has an impact, knowingly or unwittingly. As the infant is supported by the parent, so the parent gains sustenance and is subject to toxins from the world s/he lives in. Nourishment and toxins are often fused and indistinguishable (Eigen, 1999). We are permeable beings. We have psychic taste buds, psychic lungs, and are sensitive to the smell, taste, and quality of the emotional air we breathe (Eigen, 2004).

That no one is an island may be more true than we imagined. Even the feeling of aloneness that is ours all our lives depends on atmospheric conditions, including emotional atmosphere. Whatever affects our feelings, affects the tone of our existence, even our inmost relation to ourselves. As we grow, we spend a good deal of time trying to right inner skews we sense but cannot pin down. We use all the materials of the world that come our way in this labour. Too often, skews we try to right influence our efforts, throw them off, and we are left frustrated. If left undetected, warping influences spread through the social body and mushroom, perhaps reaching such a destructive climax that they finally become noticeable.

I have seen many people who feel guilty or ashamed about alone tendencies. One of the saddest things is fear of gratifying the need to be alone. The triumvirate fear, shame, and guilt permeates the self. Phrases like "I'm ashamed of myself", "I'm guilty", "I'm afraid" do more than express momentary states. They often intimate that shame, guilt, and fear are part of the I who speaks and the self it speaks about, and part of the subsoil I–me–self grow from. They act like an electric grid or barrier that makes fuller contact with oneself impossible. One would have to endure too much shame or guilt or fear to get closer to oneself.

On the other hand, a complementary and widespread problem is that too many people feel too little shame or guilt. People in high places of power often commit a whole nation to policies that benefit very few and hurt many. I shudder when I think of how high government officials in the USA gloried in the bombing of Iraq, celebrating "shock and awe" annihilation as if it were 4th of July fireworks. They acted as if smashing, murdering, and disrupting the life of another country was something to be proud of. They did not seem to grasp that people in the country they injured might have mixed feelings and that some of them might strike back. What kind of fantasy of dominance–submission drives such enactments? A demonstration that, for a time, grandiosity can blot out humanizing shame and guilt and render one insensitive to the pain of others.

Chapters Four ("Guilt in an age of psychopathy") and Five ("I killed Socrates") explore the work of guilt and related feelings in an age where an ideal of guiltless pursuit of one's interests often prevails. The word "psychopathy" pertains to states in which conscience is compromised or undeveloped or put out of play. One's concern is to win, be Number 1, to get one's way without caring about the injury one causes. It is an all too pervasive attitude. I heard of a financial high roller who has a sign on his desk: "Beware of loyalty". A warning not to be trapped by human feelings or give in to consideration of how he may hurt others in his pursuit of money and power. Affective ties corrupt the purity of his drive to stay on top unless they are ties he can use to advantage.

Chapter Four focuses on guiltless insensitivity *vs.* sensitive concern. We have an amazing capacity to be sensitive to ourselves and others and the world around us. We register the feelings of others and love the beauty of this world. But the will to power often trumps caring and gathers momentum that eludes direction and control. Concern about what we are doing to ourselves cannot be stamped out. Chapter Four explores tensions between sensitivity–insensitivity in therapy, film, and the world at large. Its inner focus is our make-up, tendencies, inclinations, modes of reflection, and imaginative expression that give us to ourselves and require cultivation. As poets and sages tell us, our main job is us, and if we fail to do better with who we are and what we are made of, we can kid ourselves as a group only so long before the hell to pay becomes unbearable and unbearably widespread.

Chapter Five takes exploration of positive aspects of guilt further. It delineates different kinds of guilt and ways guilt functions, from its practical role in regulating co-operation to deeper, even mystical awareness.

At the far end of the spiritual spectrum, attention to profound guilt opens unfamiliar domains of experience. Guilt becomes an instrument for taking us beyond itself into unexpected areas of inner freedom. At such moments, guilt burns a way to paths we did not notice, or perhaps did not exist before guilt illuminated them. Once glimpsed, we can leave guilt behind.

Chapter Six ("Revenge ethics") examines an imperative that drives us to act against our best interests as individuals and as a group. I might call this a negative flame, a stubborn and compulsive inflammation of the psyche that orders the self to risk death to avenge a perceived wrong. Jesus says if you are slapped on one cheek, turn the other. This has deep meaning beyond the obvious. It allows for time between impact and response and enables the freedom to await alternative thought, feeling, and action possibilities.

Lacan (1993, p. 6) says that one possibility in face of being struck is, "Hit me, but listen!" The point is, one need not be hemmed in by a single imperative. One can give oneself time. There is divergence of reactive thought in our beings towards peace and war. This conflict is intense in Hamlet. To speak, to listen, to bear witness, to create, *vs.* to kill oneself and others and end the tension of development. In Shakespeare's play, Hamlet opted for a regressive alternative, but laid out other possibilities that he could not give himself freedom to follow. He offered them to the future. The play, in ritual fashion, bequeaths hope of more creative attempts to work with ourselves (only not now? if not now, when?). Hamlet wants others to learn from his story. He wants not only to be memorialized, but to contribute to human reflection on our makeup, who we are, what we can do. We are a future long overdo. Can we at least pass along Hamlet's hope? Murder—literal, psychological, spiritual—is a preferred solution to difficulties to this day. Can we do a little better?

Chapter Seven ("Something wrong") and Chapter Eight ("Emily and M.E.") are in the form of dialogues between a patient and therapist, but they are more like parallel monologues, sometimes interweaving, sometimes going their own ways, streams of reverie and reflection. They give expression to life's impacts on many levels. They are concerned with lived experience and ways of responding to what most hits home. They dance around the world and self, as if circling prey, looking for ways in and out. The essential question is how to make contact with oneself, with life. How to let ourselves in, let life in.

To say that I wrote my guts out in these "parallel monologues" is not enough. I turned myself inside out every which way I could at the time. Time moves on, and several years later you live somewhere else that needs turning. It does not stop. Is it a comfort to know it keeps going when you are no longer here, that all you can do is give samples, and that you yourself are a sample? Comfort or not, it keeps going with or without you, and you work with what you can. A wild horse you cannot mount, certainly not tame, but you can feel its wind, and its wind tutors you.

"Something wrong" is the longest chapter in this book. It could be a little book in itself. It gives voice to something we feel and that humankind has thought long and hard on. We have called it sin, folly, madness, inner worm, something rotten, god knows what. Something off. Not right. A deformation, or warp, or toxin, somehow not being the right fit for oneself or for life. Not just something lacking or missing, but as if part of the self is never there and never will be there fully enough or long enough. It is the pea under the mattress only it is not a pea: it is you.

Einstein speaks of a warp in space. If space is warped, must not everything share the warp? Can we also say the reverse? If we are warped, must not space be warped, or appear to us to be so? A consonance or resonance, a fit of warps.

Pascal writes of disproportion. We are too big and small for ourselves, behind and ahead of ourselves. So many ways to try to find the thing that is off. In this chapter, I call it "something wrong". We try to right it or get rid of it, solve it somehow. But to get rid of it, we would have to get rid of ourselves. It seems built into life, *our* life. Getting rid of or blotting out is one response to our condition. To some extent, it is part of a primitive response to pain. But, with today and tomorrow's technological know-how and its great destructive ability, we had better establish better ways to work with pain. Getting rid of is not as good a model as working with. To find better ways of working with ourselves and each other: a naïve formulation for such an evolutionary challenge? In theory, we have thousands, hundreds of thousands, perhaps millions, of years to begin. Can we? Have we already?

"Something wrong" has two voices, a psychiatrist (Dr Z) and Grace, his patient. Grace had multiple psychotic breaks that required hospitalization at different periods of her life. Through her work with Dr Z and with herself, she became hospital- and medication-free. She lives close to her edge, but her edge has become her way of life. She has got better, used to herself, more self-tolerant. She is testimony that a psychotic individual can use psychosis to immunize herself from further breakdowns and live productively, value her existence, and keep dipping into and sharing it. There is a sacrament some stumble on that has to do with sharing existence with oneself, and Grace was lucky to find it.

"Emily and M.E.", like the preceding chapter, is a variant of what Winnicott calls being alone together. It is a short chapter and I am explicitly a main character. Emily and I supplement each other, often without seeming to be aware of each other's existence. Yet, it is the other mind, or psyche, or self, or being, or conscious–unconscious in the room that makes it possible for Emily and me to go where we go. Alone, very much alone, as alone as we can be, yet also with each other's presence.

While something wrong is the focus, something right comes through. Patient–therapist couples in these chapters stay glued to disturbance, bugs in the human condition. Bugs in our life are not foreign to us. A taboo truth is that life bugs us. Aliveness challenges the capacities that it gives birth to. Yet, the range of experiences grace connotes not only sweeten the pain, but touch depths of the real that give rise to a sense of mystery.

Melanie Klein (1946; Eigen, 1996, Chapters Two–Three; Eigen, 2007, Chapter Nine) handles this by positing double nuclei at the root of experience, one "bad", one "good", a psychoanalytic reworking of what, in Kabala, are called good and evil inclinations. A love core and hate core. A startling, persistent element in life is that good often feels more real than evil. Is this a sugar-coating due to over-extended idealization, a way of diminishing or blotting out pain?

Yet, individuals and religions give testimony to an area of grace that helps make it all worthwhile. Judaism speaks of the soul as pure and in contact with God. Buddhism speaks of compassion as a fundamental state of heart, wisdom as basic mind, and clear light as basic being. I do not believe this is merely wish. There may be many who testify to life's basic evil, but many testify to its goodness.

One cannot use a name without going beyond it. Areas of grace remain silently operative in lands of no-name. If one goes beyond dualities, beyond good and evil, love and hate, life and death, one is more, not less, than them.

The final chapter, "Faith and destructiveness", gives voice to basic concerns of this book and forty years of work as an analyst/therapist. It is an interview by Regina Monte in 2006, and she was able to touch and touch deeply much that is real for me because, I think, she spoke from the depths of her own reality. Real touches real, sometimes for evil, sometimes for good, often the two indiscernible, indistinguishable. This book affirms that there is something in us that works with all its might to tip the balance towards the good.

The Appendix condenses "Something wrong," focusing on extracts from Grace in the form of an extended "dramatic monologue". It was put in this form for an online feminist journal, *Moondance*, where it appeared in the Summer of 2006. I had Robert Browning's monologues in the back of my mind, but what comes out is very much of our time. Martha Frisoli Gibson added stage directions. This condensation highlights what Grace goes through being a person with this strange and amazing thing we call "mind".

CHAPTER TWO

Primary aloneness

"When the Great Bird rises very high, he must have the wind under him"

(Chuang Tzu)

Winnicott writes of essential aloneness made possible by unknown support. The baby is supported in an alone state by a not quite cognized presence. In the passages I wish to amplify, Winnicott points to an aloneness that precedes clear self–other cognition. The mother is there helping the baby, but the baby might not take in the fact that another being distinct from him is keeping him in life. Among the passages in which Winnicott feels pressed to convey this paradox are the following:

At the start is an essential aloneness. At the same time this aloneness can only take place under maximum conditions of dependence. . . .

Throughout the life of the individual there continues a fundamental unalterable and inherent aloneness, along with which goes unawareness of the conditions that are essential to the state of aloneness. [1988, p. 132]

Whether or not Winnicott's time sequences turn out to be correct, there is, I feel, an important experience he tries to express. He uses a certain verbal latitude to touch and communicate it, and I will take liberties, too. What is at stake is a psychic reality of great import, a precious piece of our beings that we must take time to live our way into and, simply, to live.

An aloneness that is supported by another one does not know is there. A primary aloneness, supported by an unknown boundless other. To think that aloneness has in its very core a sense of unknown infinite other. No wonder Winnicott says so much depends on the quality of environmental being and response. The very quality of our aloneness depends on it.

I, personally, experience something sacred in this core. I think Winnicott also did. Our lives tap into a sense of holiness connected with a background aura of infinite unknown support. That such an implicit sense is there offers no guarantees about how we use it. When the support basic aloneness needs cracks, vanishes, or is threatened, emergent self-feeling veers towards cataclysm.

Chronic self-hardening may be an important part of individuation, but a price is paid. Basic aloneness mutates, splinters, and the cataclysm one hoped to dissolve is embedded in character. We have a lot to say about character and cataclysm in ourselves and in the world, but our concern in this chapter is to support a thread of peace that Winnicott calls to our attention.

Not that Winnicott's work does not deal with catastrophic formations, but he emphasizes, in the passages I am focusing on, an Om, or shalom, or peace element that is an essential part of experience. You can see this in his calling attention to the importance of restful, quiet states in addition to exciting moments. In fact, there are ways he views rest as primary, perhaps more so than excitement. But, whatever the ordering, he considers peaceful (peacefilled) moments radically significant.

> There was an unexcited state that was disturbed by the excited one, and deserves study in its own right. [ibid., p. 114]

> These excited experiences take place against a background of quietude, in which there is another kind of relationship between the baby and the mother. We are concerned with an infant in a highly dependent state and totally unaware of this dependence. [ibid., pp. 101–102]

Quiet experience does not usually win the emphasis that excitement does. Both are important. Dissociations between them often mark trauma lines in personality. Even in optimal situations, their co-ordination is challenging. In fact, Winnicott feels health may be even more challenging than illness:

> Probably the greatest suffering in the human world is the suffering of normal or healthy or mature persons. [*ibid.*, p. 80]

> Tremendous forces are at work within the person when, as in health, they have full vitality. [*ibid.*, p. 77]

Whether "healthy" or "ill", dialectics of quietude and excitement contribute.

I remember an incident years ago when I worked at Blueberry, a treatment centre for schizophrenic and autistic children (there were children, too, who qualified as behaviour disorders on the juvenile delinquent continuum as well, although more rarely). Young people like myself in their twenties made up most of the "treatment" staff, but I have learnt there is no age limit when it comes to emotional misreading of human nature.

My memory fastens on a rare moment of peace for an autistic child. She is a beautiful girl who bears a fairy tale name like Wendy in *Peter Pan*. She climbs into a baby carriage and lies there. I happen to pass by, and am struck by the ebbing of tension in her face and body, ripples of tension flowing away, dissolving. She lies on her back, her hands up, leaving her body unguarded, a gesture of trustful relaxation. This is a girl who *must* be active, whirling, making "odd" gestures ("odd" to us, outsiders), nervous bits of movement, whorls of unknown emotional currents that do not know what to do with themselves, aches and longings and love with nowhere to go. At the time, I often thought these twitches or spasms of being were ways to drain destruction.

Now—a miracle, grace—ripples of peace move through her body and I feel peace come into mine. A young woman, bright, perky, well meaning, comes by, sees Wendy in the carriage, and exclaims, "Pooop!", poking her finger repeatedly in Wendy's chest and belly. I see ripples of startle, shock, stones thrown in clear water. Gloria, Wendy's therapist, "plays" with her. Gloria is a caring, active, good person, a strong worker, a good spirit who contributes to the élan of the place.

I had to struggle: am I seeing things? making it up? How could there be such disjunction between Gloria's and my sense of Wendy's world at that moment? Years later, after seeing Daniel Stern's and Beatrice Beebe's films of mothers needing an infant's attention, mothers actively insistent, trying to engage the infant even as the infant turns away in an attempt to tone down impact, years later, I knew that good people with good intentions experience the world like different species.

In my memory, to this day, Wendy's ripples of peace and shock continue. I witness, as if for the first time, the freezing of personality, the freezing of a person's being. My own frozen area resonates. I know how sensitive we are and how insensitive too: ripples of peace, ripples of shock, ever thawing, ever freezing.

Wendy dipped into an aloneness made possible by unknown support, a taste of boundless aloneness brought to us, in part, by who we are, an inherent ingredient of our basic nature, made possible by our implicit sense of an unknown infinite ever going on being. An unconscious background that makes it possible to relax into oneself.

I would like to make a brief detour to note the significance of some of Winnicott's terminology. The title of the chapter I am looking at is "A primary state of being: pre-primitive states" (1988, pp. 131–134). Winnicott states that inherent aloneness is a primary state. Winnicott mentions other primary states as well. For example, Winnicott writes of unaliveness appearing before aloneness: "The state prior to that of aloneness is one of unaliveness" (p. 132). Although relationships between primary states are very rich, my focus in this communication is on aloneness. Perhaps another occasion will permit further elaboration of Winnicott's network of beginnings.

In reading Winnicott, as in Melanie Klein (Eigen, 1996), expect to find a bunch of primary states. A certain fluidity of experience is expressed by Winnicott's language. To ask that it sits still and behaves is to ask the wrong question of this kind of writing. Like a psychoanalytic poem, there is a rigour here, a fidelity, a need to do justice to currents of existence as they emerge, at times emerging in the writing itself.

"A" primary state, not "the" primary state. Thus, Winnicott leaves the way open for primary states (plural), whether simultaneous, oscillating, unfolding (picture a loose, rubbery telescope, one state within or coming out of another or enfolded in each other), or a mutually permeable, multi-sided, fluxion of states.

Or perhaps in this chapter he means a primary state that extends over a number of stages (e.g., unaliveness . . . aloneness . . .), embracing a plurality of possibilities contributing to experience. Whatever the sequence, Winnicott manages to distil shades of experience important for how life feels.

Why pre-primitive? Here, he differentiates himself from Melanie Klein (1948), who writes a lot about primitive stages of mental life. For Klein, projective identification is a primitive state, stage, and mental function. Winnicott tries to get beneath this paranoid organization to something more fluid and open. If Klein calls paranoid splitting of image–emotion–object–self primitive, Winnicott calls the states he tries to convey pre-primitive, more fundamental. Winnicott feels that a good portion of what Klein describes comes later, when organizations of aggression begin to reach critical stabilization points. He feels that a lot of experiencing goes on before paranoid splitting, and that peaceful areas of experience, including benign aloneness, are crucial foundational experiences.

Winnicott can make deceptive reading. Often, his language melts like butter. He has a soft touch. Because he calls attention to delicate states of being, you do not quite realize how strong his statements are. "A primary state of being: pre-primitive stages." This is a declaration of domains that Klein's work obscures. We are in some way going further than Klein, going to places her psychology does not reach, not in the same way, not with the same focus. Winnicott tends to resituate Freud and Klein rather than lose what he feels valuable in them. But he makes no bones about the fact that he feels he is opening something crucial for living that their work misses or warps.

As the chapter moves on, he uses an oddly fetching term, "double dependence", by which he seems to mean a dependence that is even more of a dependence because it is not sensed or known. He is speaking of a very early state, but what he is communicating has implications all through life: unrecognized dependence as a greater dependence than dependence one acknowledges. Winnicott feels there is a more original dependence that eludes Freud and Klein: "the original dependence, double because not yet sensed" (Winnicott, 1988, p. 133), followed by "gradual sensing and perception of dependence". It seems as if Winnicott is saying that Freud's depiction of aggression related to dependence comes in, partly, as reaction to perceived dependence. Winnicott spotlights an earlier, unperceived dependence that supports aloneness.

Aloneness here is a positive aloneness, well being going on being. Winnicott also calls the aloneness of double dependence a "pre-dependent aloneness", part of the ground from which an individual develops. The emergence of individual experience is:

> not from an inorganic state but from aloneness, this state arising before dependence can be recognized, dependence being on absolute dependability; this state being much prior to instinct, and still more removed from capacity for guilt . . . The recognition of this inherent human experience of pre-dependent aloneness is of immense significance. [*ibid.*, p. 133]

Again, whether or not Winnicott's time sequence is correct, he attempts to clear a path to experiences important for living.

Earlier (pp. 11–12), I spoke of the baby's sense of unknown boundlessness, but in the preceding passages Winnicott writes that the dependence he touches does not sense its dependence. Neither sensing nor perception of dependence arises at this stage. Perhaps there is an implicit, rather than explicit, sense of unknown boundlessness. At some point, I feel there is. Yet, I take Winnicott to heart when he says that the point of experience he touches here does not sense dependence, even if dependence is present. To be dependent without sensing it, and to be supported in being by that unsensed, unknown dependence: this is a radical statement with many ramifications. As I live my way into it, I feel freer. To be totally supported by unknown support. There is an area of this experience that is exquisitely, thrillingly beautiful. A piece of the peace that passeth understanding. A peace that reaches towards and from the aloneness of an incommunicado core. It supports that core by its own incommunicado being. It creates a background for the history of aloneness throughout a person's life. For aloneness, too, has biography. Threads of aloneness reach forward, some of them into a "oneness of awareness". Awareness sports immense diversity but shares a common thread. The iteration of being aware, an implicit awareness of being in every speck of consciousness, is a kind of oneness, if only a oneness of something like sameness that unites human being. We love or hate our differences but one mind runs through them. One, that is, if one counts that high. All-one, all alone, all one in aloneness, brothers and sisters, shared humanity.

We grow into shared aloneness as a precious state of being, a privileged state among others, in which sharing is in the aloneness, and aloneness in the sharing. In dipping in, some of us discover new levels and qualities of caring. For some, dipping is more than enough.

CHAPTER THREE

Incommunicado core and boundless supporting unknown

A woman patient learnt I was seriously ill and one afternoon said, "I want to have sex with you. I want to know you. I want our incommunicado cores, our unknowns, to know each other."

It is hard to convey the full feeling and I do not remember everything exactly. It had to do with experiencing *everything*, nothing held back, all giving. A full "interpenetrating harmonious mix-up", but more. For a profound cognition—a deep, total knowing—was part of the mix. As if all would be involved, given, known. The unknown would be known, a known unknown. Somehow, knowing was an essential, implicit part of this unknown, the incommunicado core. Unknown to unknown, core to core. Swept up into and as everything. Everything itself.

Of course, she knew this could not happen. We would not do this; we would not hurt those close to us this way. She told me how she would "act out" sexually when she was young. Sex as a way of asserting self, tasting life, not missing anything. She had come a long way to be able to have and express her longing with me and for us to have the feel of it, to have the spirit of it.

She feared criticism. Someone would misunderstand and push her back on herself: rejection. Always the residue of being bad, that feelings that want life and are life are bad, and that she is bad for having them. Perhaps, too, she wanted to heal me. We would have this wonderful life experience and it would make a difference to both of us. It would be a moment of fulfilment, a trueness. That this would heal me was a hope, a wish, a fantasy, a caring, a feeling inside. Now, shared feeling.

I was not exactly someone she feared a critical response from. The negative someone is a kind of eternal negative someone installed in all of us, part of who we are, part of our equipment. It does many good things.

I smiled, perhaps my voice smiled, and said something like, "You're beautiful. What a beautiful feeling. I'd love it." She turned on the couch and looked at me. She was radiant. At that moment, we loved each other. Somewhere along the line I said, "I can picture it." That is, sex together. She felt a profound release.

The axe did not fall. The feeling was redeemed, validated. We could live this feeling reality as part of our birth process.

What I want to emphasize is that the known unknown remains unknown. When she said our being together would be so total that our unknowns would make contact and know each other, it was a knowing in which the unknown remains unknown. The unknown deepens, grows richer. The unknown gives birth to a fuller unknown, is part of the ever growing unknown, an unknown that is the background, horizon, and support of experience.

Winnicott speaks of an unknown core and also an unknown background. One of Winnicott's special contributions to the meaning of unknown background is that the emerging individual lacks awareness of the environment that supports it. Winnicott posits, or describes, or gives expression to, a primary state of aloneness, "an essential aloneness", "a fundamental unalterable and inherent aloneness", an aloneness that depends on the support of others of whom it is unaware. Aloneness that depends on the willingness and ability of others to adapt as fully as possible to its needs.

A statement of this condition must involve a paradox. At the start is an essential aloneness. At the same time, this aloneness can only take place under maximum conditions of dependence. Here, at the beginning, the continuity of being of the new individual is without any awareness of the environment and of the love in the environment which is the name we give (at this stage) to active adaptation of such a kind and degree that continuity of being is not disturbed by reaction to impingement of a fundamental unalterable and inherent aloneness, along with which goes unawareness of the conditions that are essential to the state of aloneness (Winnicott, 1988, p. 132).

Winnicott calls this state "a primary state of being", a "pre-primitive" stage of development. Pre-primitive partly to differentiate it from the wealth of "primitive" states developed by Melanie Klein and her followers. While Kleinian positions depend on a lot of self–other permeability, there is emphasis on the early self's defensive use of these states, where permeability readily becomes persecutory, and a me must defend itself against not-me. As I have written elsewhere (Eigen, 1996, 2006b), Kleinian psychology begins as a war psychology, psyche at war with itself and other psyches. Winnicott includes splitting (this against that) as the psyche develops, but begins as a peace psychology. There is a certain moment, central or primary, that is blessedly un-agonistic, possibly touched by the language of mysticism, the peace that passeth understanding.

Peace (*shalom*) plays a central part in ritual prayer, and I have sometimes wryly remarked that it does so because there is so little of it. The sabbath point of the soul, the peace point; sabbath, when even God can be at peace. Winnicott develops his special version of the peace point—dare I call it an area of peace?—as an important state on the way towards a larger human development, in which war plays no little part. There is so much conflict, torment, and nightmare in life that a certain peace gets drowned out, downrated. Winnicott tries to include it as a basic part of development, which may well culminate in growth of capacity to sustain the most agonistic conflicts, paradoxes, and extremes. But it is not merely defensive, not a second-class citizen. Winnicott speaks of it as *a* primary state, not *the* primary state, although there is a certain bias towards its importance for the fate of warrior components later.

Perhaps earlier and later is not the best way to speak of these things. I tend to envision a host of states succeeding and merging with each other (Eigen, 1986, Chapter Four). Perhaps, for some individuals, certain groupings are emphasized more than others and gradually stabilize out of the flow or mix as dominant and sub-dominant identities. At the least, Winnicott's "descriptions" are attempts to develop an expressive language for intuitions that beckon to him, that he finds important, that aspects of his being are based on, and that he feels are important for others. When I read Rilke, I often feel experience is born as he speaks. I would not go that far with Winnicott (or would I?), but sometimes it is something like that.

One hears echoes of Plotinus, the alone to the alone, as if Winnicott implicitly touches mystical states in psychoanalytic developmental terms. He touches what might be called a non-dualistic or pre-dualistic state, wherein a being is supported in life with a sense of continuity in time, not yet arriving at a me/not-me position. Of course, in Plotinus, the goal is rootedness in God, everything else cut away. In my adaptation of Winnicott's variant, originary, emergent being is supported by invisible, unknown God given over to adaptive care of the newborn.

Winnicott has a number of ways of referring to "the fundamental state", "the original state" (1988, p. 131). One of the most familiar to Winnicott readers is "unintegration", which he calls "unpatterned and unplanned" but not chaotic. We cannot take up a full discussion of what unpatterned but not chaotic means in this context, but wish to note that a meaning of unintegration here is a kind of experiencing prior to me/not-me duality. This is not a defensive, chaotic, disintegration effort to remain integrated and maintain identity. It is, rather, a primordial "continuity of experience of being". A sense of continuity of being in time is a primary state for Winnicott, and for its emergence and evolution it requires devoted helpers whose help remains unacknowledged as such. One might say, taken for granted, except there is not yet enough sense of discrete identities to take something for granted. Rather, the support goes on in a dedicated manner so that it can maintain the infant's continuity of experience of being without being noted as such.

Thus, Winnicott speaks of an "environment–individual set-up", in which the one cared for has no discrete notion of this care and "adaptation to need is almost complete".

The latter is indeed a forerunner, template, or, as old psychoanalysis used to say, an *anlage*, of an unknown god: a god who cares, who helps. As a psalm says, "You open your hand and satisfy the desire of every living being".

It is easy to criticize Winnicott as painting an idealized picture of care, but I fear throwing the baby out with the bathwater. There is something Winnicott is circling round that I dare not miss, something important to me and—I believe—to humanity. In trying to delineate aspects of the experiential nexus of concern, I am neglecting and taking for granted much else that goes on. We are not speaking about cognitive interactiveness, usual notions of relational intersubjectivity, ordeals, successes, and failures of mutual adaptiveness. I am assuming all this. What is at stake rather—in honing in on Winnicott's primary state—is an experiential matrix that, however described, has momentous consequences in human life. I will take some poetic liberties, but I feel that the experiential state we are touching is real.

I am positing a boundless aspect to the support that is not known, the unknown support of experience of being. Associated with Winnicott's use of the word being is living, aliveness, continuity in time, and basic aloneness supported and not ruptured. Possibly, also, a boundless aspect to the core supported, boundless incommunicado core of ongoing being supported by boundless unknown God. One could point to interpenetrating harmonious mix-up (Balint, 1968), or the interactive nature of existence, and say this devoted adaptation to the alone one is pathological. It might be, but it is also, Winnicott insists, essentially life giving.

It provides a model of care and devotion to need that is a thread of ethical sensitivity and forms a basis for the feeling of being loved in one's core (God loves me, love without bounds). We are not speaking of realistic love, which comes later (if it comes at all), but of a real love that remains alive in one's core and is challenged to undergo development as long as one lives (Eigen, 2004).

Terms that might be associated with this state, primary narcissism or autism, are often maligned, devalued, or pathologized. There is good reason for this. Acting as if one is not aware of others or not caring for the reality of others often is associated with destructive tendencies. To live in a world of one's own is a commonplace way of depicting madness, psychopathy, selfishness, lack of contact, isolation, or merely dreaminess. But there are variant uses of this language, creative autism, such as Balint (1968) touches on in his one-person relationship, an area of creativity.

If one isolates a nuclear sense that others exist for oneself (if there are "others"), to support one's life, and links this with deep unconscious boundlessness (here, especially, a boundless, supporting other of whom one is unaware), one touches a thread that characterizes all pathology. Something goes awfully wrong with the point where I am loved or ought to be loved or supported by a boundless, unknown other; an other who exists to support me, to fulfil my needs, or, with a certain twist, give me everything I want. Something gets stuck in the inner core, deep in the incommunicado core that is supported by the unknown, boundless other. In extremis, the incommunicado core itself begins to alter, turn malignant, but not without memory of radiant innocence. A surviving background or trace of sweet goodness/innocence informs some of the most malignant, twisted cores.

In psychopathy the other exists for me. Not simply to support me and feed me, but as an object to rip off, to get from what I can in this dog-eat-dog world. I have a right to kill, steal, lie, and cheat in order to stay alive. It is part of the predator–prey chain. The unknown, boundless, giving other becomes fused with a boundless taker. Ego boundlessness pre-empts the place of the giver. An existential war: one takes or gets nothing. It is up to me and me alone. Endless taking, unconscious boundlessness fused with taking. Always boundlessness somewhere, degraded, grandiose, preemptive.

Look at the rhetoric of our leaders: "shock and awe"; "preemptive strike"; display of boundless glory (the American flag is called "old glory"), obscuring the cost in lives and actual misery. A tiny bit of sanity recently prevailed as a federal court "indefinitely postponed" an offbeat display of grandiose chest-pounding called Divine Strake. The government scheduled an underground explosion of the biggest non-nuclear bomb in history on Native American land in the Nevada desert. It was scheduled for early June, 2006. Its professed aim was to see what would be needed in a nuclear weapon to mimic such a blast, or, perhaps, the other way around, what would be needed in "conventional" explosives to mimic a comparable nuclear device.

The blast was to be underground near a site that once housed nuclear tests, some eighty miles north of Las Vegas and a mushroom cloud was proudly advertised (google Divine Strake). They even named the underground tunnels divine this and divine that. Hellish, ghoulish, self-celebrating, apocalyptic imagery. Was the blast meant to intimidate Iran, to show what we will do if they do not disarm their nuclear programme? Or was it merely an imaginary (all too real) display of might to thrill and scare the populace to vote Republican in the coming mid-term election? Nothing like a show of omnipotent strength to rally the political base (a correct word, base indeed).

Native Americans, on whose soil the blast was scheduled, joined with other citizen groups to bring a suit against the federal government to stop this insanity. A pocket of sanity momentarily prevailed.

To win any way one can is corrupt enough. But add a sprinkle of boundless entitlement to the mix, an inversion of primordial, boundless support that embraces personality, and you have bottomless grandiosity. In psychopathy, a certain unconscious self-nursing function turns toxic, perversely boundless self-nursing is bound to fail (is part of Bush's "charm" charged with something of a grandiose self-nursing quality?). One unconsciously apes a supporting boundless other by becoming a boundless injuring other, a perverse boundlessness. One mimics not the support, but holes in the support, breaches, the trauma. One becomes a trauma creator, in so far as one's power allows, a mock master of injury. Injury escapes, has life of its own, and boomerangs, so that destructiveness and self-destructiveness merge (Eigen, 1999, 2001a, 2002, 2005, 2006a,b, 2007).

People all over the globe are feeling the pain of the breakdown of our unconscious supportive shield. The boundlessly good background support becomes usurped by foreground menace. People are feeling the pain of injustice all over the globe, the pain power élites push past to do what they imagine they want, uncaring. You have to think psychically to think socially. Unconscious layers of psychic support are being corrupted, eroded by maniacal poisons. In Winnicott's vision, much goes on in the psychic substratum prior to formation of an ego that fights everything. Under pressure of great wrongs, an ego geared to fight (to correct or avenge or transmute them) prematurely seizes too much personality, pre-empts boundless space, and becomes a boundless fighter. The move towards duality gets mired in this *vs.* that, always a contest. So

much so that the boundless God worshipped by so many throughout the world today is a toxic, destructive God, expressing warps in
the psychic substratum, supporting cruelty in its many guises.

As a child, the body cannot match fantasy. I should say, following Freud, as a child or as a dreamer. Almost a sweet innocence of
Freud's time, to think as sleeping dreamers it is safe to expose
(fulfil/explode) wishes. Sleepwalking hallucinations have become
blood-curdling. We have developed tools that tend towards the
possibility of a greater match between urges and fantasies of
boundless destruction and the deed itself (Eigen, 2002). The boundless supporting other has been wounded and repair is not in sight.
Deformations of the self and society spiral.

And my patient? Her love for me, her need? Her incommunicado core and boundless background other? Shall I peek at her bad
motives? She is driven by a generative boundlessness. Not only a
need to repair and to make good, but a need to create a great thing;
a great moment; a thing of beauty; a joy forever. A poignant,
wrenching, redeeming moment. A moment of suffering so huge
that it transports (in the sense of transportation) existence from one
place to another. It opens existence.

For this is where life is lived, in the affective basement everyone
feels but no one sees. It is, partly, what led Freud and Bion to give
a certain privilege to psychic reality. Bion thrillingly says that
perception of external space depends on the rise and fall of affects,
a sense of emptiness–fullness. Just as you think he is speaking
about nursing, the breast, the emptying–filling sense of milk and
nourishment, you realize he speaks about a certain affective
primacy that colours our perceptual world (Eigen, 1986, Chapter
Six).

Alone as a pre-primitive primary state supported by a background the aloneness does not know about. An implicit background in being, not a figure with conceptual clarity. Aloneness as
a sense of continuity of being in time. A maximum dependence that
is unknown supported by the boundless unknown, the latter nearly
completely adapting to the alone core.

Chaos comes when aloneness begins to disintegrate under the
impact of black winters. A traumatizing context freaks out aloneness and sets in motion a dynamic in which aloneness seeks to hide
in un-aliveness. Perhaps aloneness still hopes in un-aliveness to get

a taste of being, a hiding that is partly a waiting for being. To peek at being, to keep some of it alive, to protect it. There is too much anxiety for aloneness to let the experiencing of continuity of being grow, too much anxiety about what will happen.

Winnicott's picture of healing involves creating conditions for a valued sense of continuity of being to grow. The therapist triggers a taste of unconscious boundless support, a generative boundless unknown accessed through the medium of a somewhat known personality. A continuity that survives discontinuity, perhaps not immediately, but in time, replenishing, returning. For Winnicott continuity—not discontinuity—is primary. He does not, as is fashionable, idealize discontinuity. If anything, he might idealize continuity, but it is within an overarching experience of the continuity of being, as core and background support, embracing disruption, that aloneness seeks the riches of life.

A certain amount of self-nursing is necessary, although, for Winnicott, an early split develops between a part of the personality that is nursed, and a part that nurses. Self-nursing can be part of a positive illusion that enables one to grow. It mimics boundless adaptation to the incommunicado core. A good thing is that one can be alone with oneself, nourish oneself. But it is an illusion, an aloneness subject to shattering.

Illusion has a positive sense for Winnicott, connected with succour and creativeness. If development proceeds well from the alone core, the background boundless other stretches. Its elasticity grows into new places, trying to put a favourable turn on changing conditions and supporting living. It remains at least partly linked with roots of trust and surrender, a residue of giving oneself up to being alone with another one does not know is there.

For better or worse we are self-nursers and use others in this process. How we do this runs the gamut of addictions, perversions, power lusts (or simply lusts), creativity, love, or even ordinary daily exchanges. There remains a wish to get to primordial aloneness boundlessly supported by the other one is unaware of: a moment outside the rupturing other.

But it is not only the other that ruptures this unawareness (later, illusion). One's own development does this as well. Developmental drives perforate illusions while creating others. There are disruptive anxieties inherent to oneself, another face of aloneness.

In a somewhat idealized formulation, Winnicott asks, "What is the fundamental state to which every individual, however old and with whatever experiences, can return in order to start again" (1988, p. 131). Wishful thinking, a credo, a faith, a conviction, a vision? A genuine and incessant motor of regeneration? (see Eigen, 1992 for different kinds of rebirth experiences).

Not just a wish, but a *need* to touch base with aloneness supported by unknown boundlessness: a need to reconnect with background boundlessness that supports life. Part of a sense of trust grows out of a time or experience when one is supported without being aware of the support. When support seems a part of just being.

Whatever "pathology" or functions and uses one can read into my patient's urge and vision to sleep with me in my illness (or my acceptance and love of the beauty I felt in it), I suspect that something Winnicott touches in his credo applies. I feel the realness of her feeling vision, of incommunicado core supporting, transmuting incommunicado core, in such a way that our incommunicado cores become boundless unknowns supporting each other.

All our knowns go into the mix, fish in water, for we do know each other somewhat, in important ways, are loyal to each other, a knowing that enriches the unknown. Not "mature" adults working through conflicts perhaps, as in conflictual mutuality, not this instant. But a bit of the substratum of glory that lifts existence, dangerous, necessary, and never outgrown. Incommunicado cores and their ripples, which now and then commingle, exchange self-substances, miraculous, thrilling. Intermingling that often goes on core-to-core in muted, less intense forms. It is not that we can undo "pathology", or that pathology and analysis become irrelevant. But for the moment it is swept along in a larger current, the overflow. And something else happens. An abundance that does not fill or undo lack, but makes lack lustrous, gives wings to lack. Not only survival, a victory for caring. A moment perhaps, a moment that counts.

CHAPTER FOUR

Guilt in an age of psychopathy*

uilt: a big topic. We can take little nibbles. We can be little
fish taking little nibbles. We understand that everything we
say is partial. To say one thing, we leave another out. But
in addition to things we know but do not say, there is more that we
do not know, that we are not yet able to think, things that have not
yet swum into view, that have not yet crossed the thought horizon.
Thus, we speak humbly in face of the future, grateful to search for
the little bit we can give. Saying this, you will understand that if I
speak boldly, it is born of a pride of speech that is really a modest
portion of the immensity that touches us.

We are all killers. Thus, we are all guilty. We are all guilty killers.
There is no way around it. We cannot get out of it. We kill to live.
We kill each other to live.

* This chapter was given as a talk for the Italian Psychoanalytic Society in
Rome, April, 2005. It is part of my book, *Age of Psychopathy*, on Robert Young's
Human Nature online site: http://www.psychoanalysis-and-therapy.com/
human_nature/eigen/part1.html
Portions of this paper are based on my chapter "Guilt" in *Emotional Storm*.
Middletown, CT: Wesleyan University Press, 2005.

Killing is part of living. It is built into life. But, like light refracts into so many colours, aliveness is alive with many tendencies and counter-tendencies, many emotional colours. We kill, but are not just killers. We love, we are curious, we wonder, we explore, we drink life fully, we appreciate ourselves and each other, we appreciate the world. We care about life. We want to do life justice.

We are thus given a range of possibilities, including emotional possibilities. Something that Isaac Bashevis Singer once said is, "God gave us so many emotions and such strong ones. Every human being, even if he is an idiot, is a millionaire in emotions". In a way, then, emotion is a light we have, that refracts into many colours.

Psychoanalysis is often satirized as a kind of licentiousness. It tries to make people feel less guilty for sexuality, self-assertion, self-affirmation. Less guilty for living. Does it try to make people feel less guilty for killing? Does it try to help people be better murderers, to murder in a healthier or more productive way? To be less self-destructive killers? To be better at being bad? Does it try to help people feel guilty in more productive ways? To ignore or push past their guilt?

We are appalled by excesses of guilt, penitential guilt, extremes of masochism, self-immolation, self-suppression. We see too much guilt as pathology: neurotic or psychotic guilt. We seek to lessen the stranglehold of excessive guilt, guilt for crimes we did not commit, guilt that inhibits self, deforms, prevents, or even stops living. Guilt as a kind of suicide, a suicide substitute, which sometimes passes over into the real thing. In such extreme forms one sees the link between guilt and murder, whether murder of other or murder of oneself.

At the same time, guilt has a useful social function. It helps bind people together. It puts the brakes on murder. It is part of learning to get along with each other. It signals that we have gone too far, or are about to go too far. It is part of the way we sense each other, mould to each other, help each other. It helps modulate the way we treat each other. We would be worse without it. We have a number of modulating emotions that contribute to inhibiting aggression: shame, guilt, and anxiety among them. This is a kind of practical, evolutionary, survival view of guilt, a guilty realism.

On the other end of the spectrum, there are people who feel too little guilt; people who are guiltless when they *should* be guilty. I remember many years ago hearing the behaviourist O. Hobart Mowrer talk about his time as a patient in a mental hospital. While there, he formed small "honesty groups", "confession" groups. Patients came together to confess their sins, speak truth to each other, including whatever they felt guilty about, the bad they had done. These groups helped him immensely. He felt they played an important part in his recovery. He spoke about psychosis as a wound that fails to heal. In contrast, psychopaths were all scar tissue. He quipped wryly, "Some people just don't have the common decency to go crazy" (Mowrer, 1964).

Today, it appears that my country is run by insufficiently guilty people, people who fail to feel the horrible aspects of their actions, who keep their eyes glued to what they call self-interest, idealized as plutocratic democratic freedom. People who kill, but do not feel the effect of killing.

Perhaps they will turn out to be right. Perhaps the reality that power creates will take good turns. I cannot foresee the future. I do feel the pain of people maimed and dying in what appears to me to be an unnecessary war, an invasion as a show of might and ego, for purposes I fear to guess about. I do feel the pain of a country that may not have a successful anti-ballistic missile shield, but is walled off and suffocated by impenetrable lies. An ancient lesson of history, that guilt can be put out of play or manipulated by lying. And yet, I believe, somewhere in our psycho-social-spiritual beings, we feel mutely guilty for living a lie. A guilt that in the long run has consequences.

I suspect our time is not simply or mainly an Age of Madness but an Age of Psychopathy. More precisely: I think a keynote of our age is *the psychopathic manipulation of psychotic anxieties*. Apocalyptic annihilation and other catastrophic dreads are played and preyed upon. *They* have weapons of mass destruction. *They* are going to inflict great destruction on us. They are dangerous, predatory, evil. *We* are good. We represent freedom. We represent morality. I will not go through the list of lies and self-deceptions that led up to our invading Iraq and the way we have handled this invasion. It is an attitude that goes beyond present ghastly events. Our leaders are not the only ones who manipulate psychotic dreads to get what they want. It is a strong tendency of our economic age, among the haves *and* the have nots, and among those who profess great morality, hyper-morality.

The four-page letter found in the luggage of Mohamed Atta, one of the World Trade Center bombers, is a wonderful evocation of the goodness of destruction. To be obliterated for a godly cause is a thing of beauty and glory. Here, the USA is the evil one, the plane hijackers God's helpers. The mentor instructs Atta that soon all his disturbances will be consecrated; even his fear is holy, peace is near. Guilt is not even mentioned. It is wiped away by righteousness. The sense of being good obliterates guilt. There is no room for doubt or hesitation in the visionary approach of oneness, the marriage with God in heaven. The longed for disturbance-free state is at hand.

Shakespeare repeatedly tried to depict guilt-free evil intentionality, but invariably portrayed disturbance, e.g., Richard III's twisted mind–body; Iago as a viral parasite burrowing deep into psyche; Lady Macbeth, given to a life of murderous power, wiping bloody hands in her sleep. There are hardened murderers who feel no guilt while awake, yet are attacked by guilt in nightmares. Even psychopaths place guilt somewhere, whether out of waking consciousness into dreams, or out of self into other. Shakespeare explores guilt-free murder, but ends by portraying tormented minds. It is precisely the fact of tormenting disturbance that drives his tragic plays.

Al Pacino's recent portrayal of Shylock in *The Merchant of Venice* shocks us into awareness of the gap between Shakespeare's time and ours. Shakespeare meant Shylock to be a clown, a spectacle, a comic villain. Today, he appears more a tragic villain, linking victim with victimizer.

One can speculate what in Shakespeare forced him to find the words he put in Shylock's mouth, words that undo the play's official self-conception. Words that teach the equality of all humans before God, affirm the value of every living soul, the universal franchise of mercy. And, in virtually the next breath, words that kill, murderous, vengeful words. The victim becomes victimizer and is victimized in turn, a cycle of humiliation in which humanity is trapped.

Near the beginning of the movie we see Shylock spat at by a righteous Christian. Far from being an aberrant gesture, it was almost a Christian duty, Jewish abjection the norm. Near the end of the movie, we see Shylock grovelling in the dirt, having to express enforced gratitude for abundant Christian righteous mercy that spared his life. The "wholesome" Christians in Arden give one chills today, oblivious of the injury their top of the world self-satis-faction causes others. Shylock becomes a symbol of abjection and humiliation everywhere. The ruling Christians are branded by their presumption of superiority, the casual sense that others are not as good as they are, or worse, that the pain of others somehow does not really count. The easygoing, triumphal happiness of the self-assured is profoundly discordant with the facts of life. As if power grants innocence.

Today the "happy" ending horrifies us. Shylock's murderous desire is placed in a larger context of indignity, injustice, and enor-mous, fathomless wounds. The pressure good Christians put on Shylock to convert mocks the faith they elevate and condemns a self-satisfaction that thrives on the pain of others. Shylock shows us the underside that supports Christian prosperity. The latter looks so rich and clean as Shylock drops to the dirt in agony. This victory of Christian mercy today seems cruel and mercurial.

If we take entitlement for granted, if we kill for power, to win, to get what we want, we leave a trail of abjection in our wake, an abjection that may seek justice in whatever ways it can, including the sick compensation of revenge.

It is part of the growth of sensitivity that abjection anywhere horrifies us, in ourselves or others. We are enjoined to make life better for all humanity. Our sense of guilt is part of caring. Radical guilt, radical caring. Guilt disturbs us and we may try to play it down, moderate it, but we ought not to pretend we can get rid of it. Obliteration of guilt over injuring another is dehumanizing.

We excuse ourselves by pointing to an enemy. We say, and with good reason, "Look—they are murdering us. Why should we help them kill us?" Get them before they get us. Get them after they get us. Save ourselves, build ourselves up at others' expense. Why should we feel guilty? They hurt us, why shouldn't we hurt them? Or, in a lethal variant, "If we don't hurt them, they'll hurt us."

These are not questions that have immediate answers. They are appeals to evolve, appeals to all of us, the human group.

I wish to swerve now, take a somewhat different direction. I want to point to something more that guilt can do for us, another function, long known in religion but often mis-channelled and poorly used. I would like to say a little about the transforming value of guilt: guilt not as a way out, not an escape, but a way in. A way into contact with ourselves and the depths of others. A way into a deeper sense of life.

At the end of *Toxic Nourishment* (Eigen, 1999, p. 225), I call attention to cases in which trauma opens alternate paths of development. It can be awful, but there are instances in which

> deep lines cut by trauma provide access to depths that are otherwise unreachable. In such instances, nourishment follows trauma to new places. We wish things could be otherwise . . . easier. But we have little choice when illumination shines through injury.

Guilt as torment, as a disturbing force, can puncture the psyche, creating apertures for new kinds of experiencing. It is an amazing fact, for some people, some of the time, that intense torment perforates walls of the psyche, opens the soul to awesome, delicate feelings, psychic sensations and awarenesses, impalpable, ineffable regions of being that leave one breathless, at once elusively tantalizing, uplifting, and sweet. If one follows the arc of this movement far enough, aesthetic responsiveness touches ethical responsiveness, perhaps a touch of what Keats saw when he brought truth and beauty together in poetic vision. What opens, deepens, challenges us, is a filling out of sensitivity, not only to touch, colour, sound, line, or space, but to self and other. A spontaneously meaningful urge to do well by oneself and others, to do justice to life, in so far as one can. A guilt that gets absorbed by caring.

I would like to take a somewhat deranged detour, using Ludwig Wittgenstein, not exactly as a case, but as an example, a testimony of the power of guilt as a kind of psycho-spiritual wormhole one enters, then finds oneself emerging somewhere else, far from where one started, in places one knew by hearsay or did not know at all. We could pathologize his journey but I want to bring out something more. Wittgenstein had three brothers who killed themselves and a sister whom he sent to Freud: you can imagine the forces he had to deal with in order to survive. Not only to survive, but to thrive as a thinker, to enjoy his talent as an architect, to live and have a share of loving.

As a young man, Wittgenstein went through a period in which he felt compelled to confess his sins to people he knew. He *had* to say everything bad he felt himself to be. I suspect he imagined that if he could only say enough, communicate his guilt fully enough, that he could be free of it, reborn, fresh, a new being. I think he imagined that he could get rid of sin by talking about it.

Confession certainly has its values, as does talking oneself out, revealing to others what festers in inner abscesses. Speaking from the place of hidden infections can help. But the infection of self does not go away. One does not end evil by talking about it. Shakespeare and William Blake tell us repeatedly about a canker, a worm within that will not go away. But there *are* better and worse responses to it. Perhaps our biggest job of all, our greatest calling, is to discover, to seek, to find better responses to ourselves.

Wittgenstein's interest in religion was not merely academic. It had to do with living, how to live life, something that came from within. Wittgenstein spoke of three kinds of experience that might be termed religious, or that religious life draws on. One is wonder that the world exists, an experience of the miracle of existence. Another is a deep sense of safety, "the calm bottom of the sea at its deepest point, which remains calm however high the waves on the surface may be" (Wittgenstein, 1984, p. 53). The third is "absolute guilt" (Brenner, 2001, p. 57). This last is associated with God's judgement, a judgement that runs through us with regard to how we feel and act towards each other, a shudder of disgust we have at things we and others do. Feeling absolutely guilty is a ganglia with many filaments. It moves in many directions, opens many channels.

One filament or channel is Wittgenstein's (1984, p. 48) sense that "only religion would have the power to destroy vanity and penetrate all nooks and crannies". A sense that there is some psychical, spiritual something that has to do with goodness that penetrates all nooks and crannies. Human beings have sensed hidden nooks and crannies for a long, long time. In the psalms, God searches secret spots, intricate invaginations of our being. We ache for this search, for this knowing because we are hidden from ourselves. We long to be known, to be felt, to be experienced. That God permeates us is scary, even terrible, but it is a grace, a source of love as well as fear. Through this permeating grace, we feel a sense of infinite, intrinsic value through and through.

To be penetrated this way, like a lamp lighting paths in a complicated mine, ignites struggle. One gets glimpses of who one is, the sediment, the nastiness, the vanity, the love. If one cares enough for the other, one struggles with oneself. One holds back, tempers one's temper so as not to injure. For feelings *can injure* and *be injured*. People are injured. Psychoanalysis has been criticized for dwelling too much on injury, but we still are far from integrating our sense of being wounded–wounding creatures into the social body.

A few years ago, I heard a good politician who lost a campaign say that he severed his nerve endings a long time ago. He was inured to injury. He severed his sensitivity to pain in order to function as a politician. At least he had some awareness of a price he paid for the life he chose.

Today, my country has a head of state who feels he must look strong at all times.[1] He must not show weakness, admit error, and certainly not feel or show guilt. Politicians have long known they must choose between injuries and take the injuries that seem the better course. Guilt is secondary to the exercise of power. You cannot win if you feel too guilty about what you have to do to win. We have enormous capacity to maximize and minimize guilt, depending on complex contexts.

Wittgenstein tended to maximize guilt. This does not mean he never split guilt off, played it down, ignored it. There certainly were times that his wishes and drives pushed past guilt. But he was not inured, not immune. He wrestled with guilt. He acknowledged guilt's claims. He acknowledged the fact that guilt carries important messages about the self, about how one lives, and who one is, or should be, or can be.

Some may think he overdid it, and that might be so. He turned down positions and publication offers out of a misplaced sense of integrity. But, when we think of the philosophical and psychological junk foods that pollute our psycho-sphere, the flood of stuff that comes at us for economic and egocentric gain, we may view his misgivings with a more kindly eye, even with nostalgia.

We know that guilt can be cancerous, stifling. Guilt infuses pseudo-morality, moral tyranny, murderous superego. It is, as so much is, Janus-like, depressing life, opening possibility. Guilt is cruel, persecutory, inhumane, pitiless, demoralizing. Yet, it can be humanizing, allied with sensitive caring. It contracts us, narrows us, pierces through our hearts, brings us to deeper places.

Now, at this moment of history, I would like to say a positive word for certain aspects of guilty torment and self-doubt. There are ways that tormenting guilt and self-doubt can be friends and helpers, goads for growth, signals of horror. For example, parents who rage and discover they are damaging their children. Raging parents who become horrified at what they do to their children and recoil in self-doubt and grief. Few things injure a child more than parental rage.

I have worked with many parents who love their children, but rage at the drop of a hat. Almost always they feel right or righteous. The child is wrong about something, has misbehaved, broken a rule, tested a control or boundary. Rage comes in a blinding flash, yet there are micro-steps that lead up to it. Rage has preparatory signals, much as an epileptic seizure does. One "knows" one is going to blow up and there are a number of choice points along the way that are ignored. The feeling mounts like an angry orgasm, and one fails to exert force against it.

Many parents feel ashamed and guilty afterwards, as one might after masturbating. Many keep justifying themselves, pushing counter-feelings away. Some even justify raging at infants, parents who yell in exasperated fury at a screaming infant. Rage tries to shut the other up, stifle the screams of others. Perhaps one tries to scream loud enough to drown out the appeal, demand, or distress of the other, even if the other is a baby.

Therapists are privileged to learn what happens in micro-moments. In my book, *Psychic Deadness* (1996, Chapter Twelve), I write about a man who recalls a moment when he died, i.e., when his feelings numbed, froze. It was after an unexpected paternal rage, a capricious rage at dinner over something trivial, something that had no value except in the parent's imagination. The patient recalls shock, momentary trembling, then a spreading psychic anaesthesia which never fully went away. He lived on the other side of this frozen state ever since.

Someone might say, "Get over it, get on with it. Why dwell on things like that?" My patient became a successful man, and lived a full enough life on the other side of the freeze. But he came for help to reclaim himself, to thaw out. In a secret, important way he felt he was a corpse who wanted to live. We all die, to some extent, in order to live, to survive. Psychic deadness is part of life. But perhaps some of us die more than we have to, in worse ways than necessary. Some of us hope that, with help, we might find more life.

There are many intimate connections between rage and guilt. Rage can obliterate guilt. Guilt sometimes tries to stifle rage and sometimes succeeds, but often fails. The rager refuses to be imprisoned by guilt. There is a boundlessness in rage that carries special satisfaction. Few experiences feel more total than all-out rage.

Guilt adds seasoning to lesser rages, akin to an alcoholic feeling guilty and ashamed after a binge, swearing he or she will never do it again. The addiction is too strong, the build-up too compelling. In such a case, guilt adds flavour to the brew, but fails to hold the storm back. In some instances, rage inflames itself in order to obliterate guilty whispers. Someone may rage in order to have something to feel guilty about. Very often the rager expects the one raged at to feel guilty, a common division of labour. The rager tries make the one raged at feel bad, intimidates the one raged at to be the carrier of guilt.

In therapy, it is often not enough for the rager to gain understanding of his or her condition. At some point, after enough empathic understanding and assuaging of injury, the rager has to struggle with him or herself. The rager has to see and feel the injury he or she is mediating, to see and feel that he or she is a traumatized traumatizer. The parent has to feel the impact she has on the child she loves.

It is very difficult to hold oneself back in face of a flood of feelings. Often one fears one will damage oneself by holding back the storm. Some fear they will be destroyed by inner whirlpools. I have heard many people say, "I'm afraid the feelings I hold in are damaging my insides." Some feel helpless in the face of guilt, or fear sinking into the latter, convinced that giving in to guilt will cause them harm. Little by little, therapy supports the still, small voice that says there has to be a better way.

It is important to learn that there are ways of gripping oneself, holding oneself tightly, pulverizing oneself, that open new pathways of experience. There is suffering and guilt that may diminish existence, but there is suffering and guilt that leads to greater life. Guilt varies in its function. In the case of many ragers, guilt needs all the support it can get. Guilt and sometimes fear: one needs to be afraid of what one can do to others. Like porcupines, we need to learn to modulate our quills when we are close.

I fear we are living in a time when the consequences of our actions are not keenly felt. We do not want to feel them, lest they slow us down and make us wait and become uncertain. If we slow down too much, someone else will beat us to the goal.

To drown in guilt is one pole, to be monstrously guiltless another. In human life, there is no contradiction between loving music and children, and sending the latter to the beat of the former to die in the name of the fatherland and motherland. A fused pair, the indignity of trauma and vanity of power.

Wittgenstein is not afraid of trying to put torment to good use. Of course, he blunts it, escapes it like everyone else. After trying to engage an area of thought or being in a class, his exhausted, drained state leaves him good for little except staring blankly at a movie. But he affirms the value of guilty torment in principle, and lives it to the extent he can. He sees through the idea of a super-race, entitled group, or an idealization that places the condescension of health and wealth above those who suffer. Compassion is for equals. A fraternity of sinners is grounded in empathy. We are equals in guilt towards one another. The heart of the other calls for a caring gesture, but we have a habit of looking the other way. To help another is costly, but not to help is more costly.

Absolute guilt never tires of calling for a response. It is a guilt we share, that obligates us to one another, a challenge requiring the use of all we are and have. It brings us to places we could not have imagined had we asked less of ourselves. Guilt sticks to us, pressures us towards a loving heart, intensifies appreciation of self and other, and heightens awareness of our preciousness. Guilt calls us to live more fully, to wed other with self, self with other. A wedding nourished by the profundity of difference.

Sometimes, when I read Wittgenstein on guilt, torment and suffering, I think of Flannery O'Connor's portrayal of Hazel Motes in *Wise Blood*, an erstwhile "saint" who wore barbed wire under his coat, a barbed wire inside us. A torment more part of the human than many would like to believe. For Hazel Motes, suffering contracts to a point of light, vanishing in the infinitesimal infinite. For Wittgenstein, suffering, if related to rightly, calls us out of disappearance, awakens us, moves us to be of use.

For Wittgenstein, too, there is a gravitational pull from guilt to God. There is, of course, plenty of meaningless suffering in the world. That is not what is at stake here. Wittgenstein locates and tries to share something that happens through suffering guilt fully. He bears witness to an experience: intense guilt can lead to God. Intense suffering can lead to God. Of course, intense suffering can make us loathe God, deny God, render God irrelevant. But it also can link us to each other and to God.

Wittgenstein (1984, p. 86):

> Life can educate one to a belief in God. And *experiences* . . . are what bring this about; but I don't mean visions and other forms of sense experience which show us the 'existence of this being,' but, e.g., sufferings of various sorts.

Experiences, sufferings of various sorts force God on us. In this context, we are not debating whether or not God exists, or about particular details about his nature or our relationship to him. We are not asking what is possible. We are expressing what is.

We express God a little like we express pain. We might have less doubt about pain. But when suffering brings us to God, doubt is not what we are about. Nor are we about bludgeoning others with God, forcing our God on others. We are with God with our suffering. Not teaching a class, fighting a war, or making conversions.

A result of reaching God through suffering is renewed struggle with self. Suffering shows us something wrong with ourselves, a way of being, a propensity we are guilty about. We are suffering, in part, because we are guilty about our way of life. We live from a place where there is a connection between suffering and ethics. An ethics of caring, not phoney morality to get one's way. It is precisely the latter that is one of the things we struggle with.

Two people moving a filled-to-tipping wheelbarrow across a bumpy terrain rely on mutual sensing to get from here to there. It is not something one thinks out. An implicit intelligence gets the feel of the load, terrain, and partner, modulates subtle movements to shifting factors as one goes along. Guilt plays a modulating role in getting along together as a relationship moves from here to there. It is part of a larger field of social sensing, self-to-self sensing, spontaneously adjusting volume, intensity, affect colouring as we move along.

Therapy is one kind of wheelbarrow, marriage another. People bring marriages to therapy when the movement goes awry and teamwork fails. A man in his fifties, after spending much of his adult life in therapy, finally was able to marry, only to discover that his wife would not be bullied. He got away with being a bully in his marriage for a while, as he did most of his life. One wonders what happened in all the therapy he had.

He was helped to make a go of it, to become successful and *not* be impeded by guilt and anxiety. Therapy enabled him to push past guilt and anxiety on his rise up, but he was not very much helped to live intimately with another human being. Work substituted for intimacy. Life permitted him to skip around very real emotional disability. He came to see me for help with his marriage, which I soon realized meant helping him manage his wife. The idea of working on himself, struggling with himself, was a foreign notion, unless it meant figuring out how to achieve a goal. He imagined marriage would fall into line like a business problem.

He filled the room, shining with success, confident I would help him with his wife in no time at all. His time sense baffled me. He spent years in therapy. He must know that it is anything but instantaneous. He is a good businessman. Surely he must know something about timing. He smiled at me and made reassuring hand gestures, which made me feel he was nervous but could not say so. Clearly, he was a man used to getting his way.

He painted a picture of his wife. She was depressed, moody, irritable, a workaholic like he was, except that he was steady as a rock, imperturbable. What is wrong with her: she gets upset too easily. He pointed his finger as if she were sitting there and said several times, "Something is wrong with her."

Recently she has got moodier, bursting into rages, criticizing him, distancing herself, withdrawing into her study. "I don't like being with you," she would say.

"She must need different medication," he decided. His worked, why didn't hers?

I once wrote half a book (*Reshaping the Self*, 1995) about a businessman who approached therapy like a financial project. Over time, he learned to switch gears to give the psyche its due. To sense what is happening of emotional importance is a capacity that is hard for many people to contact. One gets used to ignoring it for the sake of other gains. In his case, realization of how his children, as well as himself, were injured by his way of life got through to him.

The high-powered man who came to see me to fix his marriage was used to putting his wife down. He did not even know he was doing it most of the time. It took less than ten minutes of his first visit for me to learn that he made all the major decisions in their lives. He expected her to fall into line and appreciate the great life they led. His wife increasingly reacted against a depreciating, humiliating attitude he took for granted. Speaking to him did not work. He did not listen. She stood up to him in the only way she could, by being difficult, moody, and nasty. Her feelings broke through the medication.

His seeing me was an attempt to maintain control. She wanted them to go to couples therapy and he refused. He feared the thera-pist would side with her and call him to task for his bullying nature. For him, it was a simple fact that he felt best on top, a boss. A posi-tion of dominance worked for him. Couples therapy was too threat-ening. He was used to making believe his marriage was better than it was. It became nearly constant war, though they still loved each other.

He was short-tempered with his children as well. He expected to be listened to, even though he did not spend enough time with them to develop a relationship. He thought his position as a father was enough. He did not have a painful enough sense of what he was missing, although he knew he was missing something. At first, he did not relate his children's problems to the atmosphere at home, but soon developed at least a vague sense that there was some connection between his life and theirs.

There was little or no guilt involved in his capitalist notion of family life. As if it were up to each person to fend for him- or herself, without sufficient provision of interconnected support. He had not yet reached the real struggle with himself. He was light years away from that kind of pain, although there were glimmers. I felt it a victory when he finally agreed to go to couples therapy and risk exposure. He had a dawning inkling that capacities he needed to be with another person, a wife, a marriage, a family, had not developed, or had taken a negative turn. To admit that he feared exposure as emotionally illiterate was a start. His marriage and behaviour needed airing out, a fresh look, a caring, objective presence. Going to a couples counsellor might be like opening a window. And it would be listening to something his wife wanted.

"Where was the guilt?" I wondered. Vanished in entitlement? Vanished in the trauma and humiliation that others carry for him? Did he make others feel guilty and ashamed for not being strong enough, good enough, able enough, happy enough for him? Was he a kind of predator who preyed on others' insufficiencies, intensifying and manipulating their weak spots? Was there a murderous hole where guilt should be, a marauder's sense that life should not resist him? Perhaps there was no place for effective guilt in his life, because there was no developed way for him to appreciate the reality of his affect on others. Perhaps there were ways in which other people were not fully real, except as ways to get things. To treat another as an end in itself, a precious subject in her own right, was not what he was about. The threat of his marriage breaking up and his children not caring about him, the disturbance they and his wife were making, showed signs of breaking through.

To begin to notice that things were worse than he thought and that he lacked ability to respond as others needed was, at least, a preliminary gesture towards self-confrontation. It would take quite a difficult gestation before he realized that a response he could not give was pressing to be born. For most of his life, he had not even known that such a pressure exists. To help shepherd this pressure is partly a function of positive, creative guilt, a personal expression of the realization that, in the realm of intimacy, no one can substitute for what we, and only we, do for each other. To what extent this "big" man, this "winner" can achieve such a realization remains to be seen. It is a problem important for our larger society, as those who exert control over the economic course of things have telling effects, the attitudinal context of their lives not the least of their impact.

Another individual, an artist, who felt himself to be a "loser", had grandiose expectations that partly fuelled his art. As a child, he felt admired, cared for, supported. He frequently complained in therapy, "My childhood was too easy. It gave me a false picture of life." Perhaps his sense of childhood ease was semi-idealized. He always felt different. To be set off from others because of talent is a source of praise and admiration, but also makes one sort of freaky. He once said, "When I was a kid and saw trapeze artists at a circus,

I thought, that's me. Up there, colourful, everyone staring, eyes upward as I take risks, fly from ring to ring, colour to colour, subject to falling at any moment. Wonderful, yes, but set off from everyone except other trapeze artists. And, as you know, artists are mainly preoccupied with themselves."

Life tempered his grandiosity. He met with moderate success, was respected, made a decent living. Not the great star high above. He had to content himself with digging in and working his work as one among many who felt different as artists. It might be that we live in a time when everyone who is not a big executive or big artist feels a little like a loser. One is overshadowed by those above, the ones who really have *it*. Life throws the success of others in one's face and one has to settle, make do, find something that works well enough. Artists stake claims to special territories that differentiate them from other artists, only to discover that different is not so different after all. One has to scale down and give oneself more and more fully to what one *can* do, to stay with the work, and keep on staying with it because it is there, because it is what one does, and it is more than enough to make life feel worthwhile.

There is a subtle, underlying guilt in all this. The guilt of being different, but not being different enough. Do artists feel guilty for being artists? Do they funnel into art a more generic guilt attached to being human? To feel anxious or guilty as an artist can deflect one from more general difficulties one can not grasp.

It is a credit to my patient that he persisted in his work in spite of what life had in store for him. In his teens, his father died, followed by his mother's permanent hospitalization for psychotic illness. Art held him together, albeit shakily for many years. He suffered breakdowns periodically much of his adult life. He broke down after his first child was born, after an affair with a favourite model, after his first grandchild was born. He came to see me because he meant to kill himself and felt enormous guilt over letting down his children and grandchildren.

Some might say that the guilt itself helped to provoke suicidal impulses, but it also played a role in keeping him alive. Nothing lit him up like his grandchildren. He pictured what they would feel if he killed himself. He owed them more than that. He owed his children more.

He felt guilty for letting his children down as they were growing up. He was preoccupied with his work and did not give them
the support they needed. His wife was a rager and traumatized
them on a daily basis. The smallest, stupidest things would throw
her into an uproar and he would go on working in his studio. He
ignored the crying, the screams, shut his ears, persevered. He had
all he could do to keep himself together. He felt guilty and the guilt
mounted, but there was nothing he could do about it.

He told me over and over, "I'm a bad person. I'm bad." He meant
by this sins he dare not reveal, bad things he did that he lived with,
that haunted him, scarred him, drove him mad. One thing was
putting his penis in a baby's mouth. It is difficult to say why he did
such a thing. Was he trying to feel clean, hoping that contact with
freshness would make him fresh? Was he trying to corrupt innocence, to spoil something good, create a drama to see whether
good or evil would win? Was he trying to heal himself? Was he
trying to feel big? Was he trying to be a god? Was he trying to
reverse trauma, to do to a baby what was in some way done to
him? Was he trying to feel as important as a nursing nipple, a source
of life? Was he identifying with a baby being traumatized by an
insensitive, invasive other who stuffs unwanted life down its throat?

He has been expiating these acts ever since. Madness and suicide as partial expiation. Perhaps there was guilt beneath his childhood he did not know about, part of the parental atmosphere. Not
exactly secrets parents kept from him, although that also was the
case. He knew his father suffered persecution in Europe before
coming to the USA, and endured horrors he would not talk about.
Guilt threads through personality, guilt for who one is and fails to
become, for what one does and what survival forces one to do,
aches over transgressions one does not even know about, plus
opaquely sensed remorse one keeps tucked away. One can never
catch up with and lay bare all that one feels guilty about, or should
feel guilty about. There are times when one feels guilty for not feeling guilty about bad things life forced one to do. Rich and poor
amalgams of guilt and shame and pride.

Old formulations say we are born into guilt and suffer each
other into being, as if guilt antedates us, awaits us, and we find
ways to oblige, to supply it with subjects and objects and give it
narrative form. *My* guilty story, *your* guilty story. When my patient

says he put his penis in a baby's mouth so he could have something concrete to feel guilty about, I suspect he is not entirely wrong. It is a vicious circle, since his action scarred him for the rest of his life, gave him something he will never stop feeling guilty about. At the same time, he gave a more formless sense of being bad a local habitation and a name. To be bad for this or that reason seems better than just being bad. Nevertheless, crimes against the self do not do the trick. The sense of badness persists.

A profound self-hate in personality is a central part of what we work with. In *Turtles Can Fly*, a movie by the Iranian director, Bahman Ghobadi, about children in Kurdistan on the eve of the American invasion, the protagonist, a resourceful boy, nicknamed Satellite, falls in love with, or is fascinated by, a winsome girl, who a Jungian might feel is an aspect of his anima. Satellite tells her hopefully, "I've been waiting for you for years."

As the movie unfolds, we see that she and her brother care for a young boy left parentless by war, and we see a flashback in which Saddam Hussein's soldiers raped her repeatedly. She fears the boy will be stigmatized as a bastard when he gets older, and her own stained status as a rape victim will haunt her life. To say she is angry with her fate would be an understatement. A mixture of pride, anger, despair, shame, guilt, hopeless beauty: the weight of the way society works or fails to work, war, blindness, helpless power, children without parents living in caves and abandoned vehicles, a life too hard and impossible. I suspect Satellite's forward-looking hope excited her greater despair, and she killed the child and herself. Life symbol becomes death symbol. The best and the worst go on simultaneously.

Ghobadi is portraying a version of something real: awful living conditions, social ignorance, social pressures, sick biases of the human mind and body, rape, a sense of banishment, humiliation, caring, the pain of what we do to each other, building lives. All this in a most beautiful mountain setting, encompassing human spoilage. I want to turn or twist this movie for my purposes, lift the girl's spin into death out of context, because I think it is something very real inside us, something more universal than we tend to grant. It is a spin into death, a suicidal impulse or gradient or impulse or urge. Freud called it death drive and made it quasi-biological, a move that gets discredited.

And yet it is there, this spin downward, whether in blue moods, crashes, depressive tendencies, energy loss, or the need to space out. Often it is part of recovery, a dying out preparatory to coming back and regaining impetus. We have an unconscious urge to kill ourselves, attack ourselves, cut ourselves to pieces, to pulverize everything inside, an urge partly mediated by guilt. I sometimes get an image of banging spices in a mortar and pestle, pulverizing our ingredients so that they recombine into something better or different or simply another taste. We are curious about all the ways we can taste ourselves and may go to extremes of self-grinding in order to squeeze out another possibility.

Satellite was a resourceful, productive aspect of personality, organizing homeless children in the service of survival, on the side of work and love. The girl who killed the child and herself (she reminds me of the heroine in the old movie, *Black Orpheus*, whom death follows and inhabits) is something more resourceless in us, something that goes under in face of life, that, finally, succumbs to trauma and a sense of impossibility. She drowned the child and jumped off a beautiful cliff. To go under, to fall, to never stop going under, drowning, falling, this is a soul movement with no end in sight. A soul movement power exploits, occludes, debases. We need to make room for it.

Binaries of those above, those below, victims and victimizers, exploiters and exploited are played up or played down by social structures and policies, and need to be addressed on a societal plane. But such structures are constituted by us, by human beings trying our hand at living. Our psyches have something to do with the kinds of social forms that evolve. There is no society without psychic forces and we will not learn to work with ourselves better without taking the kinds of beings we are into account. Society is dependent on psyche as well as moulds it. No matter how good we are to each other, there will still be a murderous impulse in our midst, and, with murder, guilt. If we want to better the way we live, we have to work on many planes at once.

There are at least two main modes of relating to feelings, two attitudes. We can relate to our feelings in a caring way. I can care about what you and I feel, whether we are together or apart. We can also use feelings as signals for manipulation. I can try to manipulate your feelings for my own schemes and aims, to get what I want at your expense, for dominance, control, to win. At one extreme is cold psychopathy: relentless, remorseless use of affective cunning for gain, for power. Another extreme is the saint who puts the welfare of others first. We are a sneaky, cruel, and caring group. Both tendencies intertwine, double helixes of the psyche. Guilt can function to bring us closer, to steer us towards each other and bring caring to new places. It is a positive quality, part of a tendency to help, to nourish, to give. We have learned a lot about how hypocritical we are, all the ways we use so-called good qualities as screens for cunning, as propaganda tools. But this does not mean that goodness is not good. Our wish to help is not always or mainly hostility or servility in disguise. At the same time, it would be jejune to underestimate our callous natures and positive and negative aspects of the will to power.

Our need to help, to nourish, is a profound and vital part of our nature. But not the only part. We would not be here today if we were not so variant. It is difficult to cognize our vast discordance, what Pascal pointed to as our disproportion with ourselves. That we are cruel killers. That we are caring lovers. That we nourish and destroy. That we are guilty, that we are guiltless. It sometimes seems that we hurt each other so that we can help each other. Is there such a thing as nourishing gestures free of wounding components? Is that, in part, what we mean by grace?

When I was young, I would find alternating blends and colours of light compelling. They sent chills of beauty up and down my spine. That experience has evolved and deepened into a sense of interweaving of alternate attitudes, marked not just by thrilling beauty, but something more horribly dumbfounding and blood-curdling. Multiple affective currents, simultaneously co-present and alternating, span many domains. Our alternating, mixed affective attitudinal field is one of our greatest evolutionary challenges.

What kinds of partners with our capacities can we become? We cannot keep up with what we do. But the way, the tone, and spirit in which we lag behind or get ahead of ourselves is important. We need to grow in capacity to work with disproportion.

We face pockets of undefined immensity and much destructive gluttony. The latter seems to be part of aliveness. A focus of psychoanalysis is how destructive we are to ourselves and each other. Freud (1937c) spoke of a force against recovery. Melanie Klein

(1946, p. 297) spoke of a destructive force within. Wilfred Bion (1965, p. 101) spoke of a force that goes on working after it destroys time, space, existence, personality. We have grown to the point, some of us, some of the time, of recognizing the grip destructive tendencies have. A lot of components go into destructive urges. We know very little about their makeup or what to do with them.

Biblical injunctions to give to the poor and weak and needy recognize realities of power. Biblical stories locate the difficulties not just in social structures, but in each one of us. For if none of the current dominance structures existed, we would create them or something like them. They grow from our own natures, our psychosocial tendencies. The will to power has its own impetus. But so does a caring consciousness, a will to help where help is possible. A need to tug at the boundaries of what we can do.

We can try to imagine a person who does not help another all life long. We are fascinated by such demonic portrayals in literature. We imagine people who wilfully try to extirpate all vestiges and signs of altruism as a matter of principle. We depict a cold, indifferent ruthlessness that is an aspect of our beings. From such an attitude, helping another is anathema or, at best, an acquired taste. One has to push oneself to get out of oneself, to extend a helping hand. Patients coming from such a place may dream of corpses coming to life when feelings begin to thaw. But there are, too, many of us who would starve inside, if we could not feed another.

We may not know what to do with our caring, cruel beings, but it is our turn to try. We should feel guilty if we do not try to do a little something, to push an edge or nibble at a boundary, or let a creaky hand reach out.

Note

1. This chapter was written before the change to the current, 2009, administration in the USA.

CHAPTER FIVE

I killed Socrates

'

"I killed Socrates." I woke up this morning with these words on the tip of sleep. Did they wake me up? Will they wake me up? Can I be woken up at all?

How can I be of service to the dreamer, a dreaming me dreaming a waking dream? I do not remember being asleep when it dawned on me that I killed Socrates. I am sure I was not asleep. Yet an electric charge carrying deep conviction jolted me awake. I realized I must spend the day's best time letting in this new fact. Now that I know I killed Socrates, there is no going back.

Is killing Socrates my life's mission? I am not so sure. But I think I should try to find out why I killed him *this* time.

"All men are mortal. Socrates is a man. Therefore, Socrates is mortal." A syllogism from freshman year in college. Do you believe it? What basis does it have in fact? Is Socrates really mortal? It seems a little unbelievable, something one must find out for oneself.

As part of my scientific investigation, I sneaked up on Socrates just before dawn and strangled him, gripping his neck from behind. I dared not see him and could not bear the thought of him seeing me at the moment of murder, just before death. I repeatedly stabbed him in the back and beat him with sticks and stones. When he was down I kicked his body mercilessly. Then did the whole thing over again, and again, until I convinced myself that nothing was left other than a lifeless body. I killed him until no doubt about his mortality remained. Murder as a solution to radical doubt. Proof that death is real, an irreducible fact, deeper, more final than doubt. But is it?

I had not taken two steps from his body before it hit me that Socrates *is* immortal. His ideas never die. His thinking, Plato's thinking, play an essential role in the way we think, permanently affect how we think, what we think about, play a role in structuring thought for hundreds and thousands of years. No mind is unmarked by Plato, no mind unscathed by an Idea of the Good. Those who run from it or degrade it are broken by it. Is anything more powerful?

Yet, it is, after all, the figure of Socrates that most attracts me. Is that my peculiarity? Like water, I run through Plato backwards to the source. How odd a thing to say, given that Plato is the source, the author, the creator of Socrates. Such a convincing creator that we deeply feel that Socrates is the true author.

How to fathom that Socrates is a fiction? Or perhaps a fact Plato draws from, a man who lived, a teacher, who like a *Totem and Taboo* father, grows more compelling through death, through the fact that we, the sons, murder him?

Is it that Socrates the man, the thinker, the personality enabled Plato to become the seeker and thinker he could be, precisely because the impact of mind to mind is not confined to the literal touch of bodies? Socrates' mind and the way he approached mind released Plato's will to think. Or is it that Socrates as an imaginary nucleus egged Plato on, mental fire that does not stop burning?

Let me confess I am turned on by Socrates. It is Socrates I love, Socrates I am drawn to. It is Socrates, not Plato, who is alive in me today. Alive after I killed him. More alive the more I kill him.

I am grateful to Socrates for surviving my acts of murder; so grateful I can cry.

I am also grateful, a lesser gratitude, to Plato for giving me Socrates. Although I admit this begrudgingly, without Plato, there would be no Socrates for me to love. Without Plato, there would not be *this* Socrates, the one he vividly creates. It is, of course, a measure of Plato's amazing triumph that I love Socrates more than him, that

Socrates truly matters more, that it is not Plato I love at all, but Socrates who claims my being.

I *know* Plato matters more to the history of thought, but I *feel* Socrates matters more to the history of life. Socrates is part of the history of imaginal being, a history of inner fire. A wondrous fire my tiny spark of being participates in. Who are we that a creation of one man's imaginative daring touches lives of others over thousands of years?

For a time (is it still that time?), putting Plato down was a fad. His thought forms free and freeze us. We fight them, move through them, liquefy and burn them. We try to escape. Some of us almost get away or claim to, make end runs, see through them, and try to begin somewhere else. Some throw stones, denigrate them. It is important to bring out shortcomings, circumscribe false directions, reset the compass.

At the same time, I savour Socrates, his being, his realness. Perhaps more than his thinking, the questions Plato puts in his mouth and ideas that arise, is his being. What most touches my essence is an affective attitude, a hunger for truth, an insatiable need. His dedicated insatiability and persistence strikes a great sound within which, once sounded, never stops.

Socrates is depicted as homely, even ugly, yet his passion and beauty of spirit ignite kindred passions in others through the ages. For Socrates, intellectual drive commingles with grace, irony, humour, love. He bites and draws blood, but it is a bite we long for. Yet, I killed him. And I am not the only killer. My ancient Athenian peers—we are all peers—began this murder and we continue it.

It is difficult to admit that murder is part of the transmission of thought, that murder structures mind and soul to this day, that murder makes mind more alive. At the same time, thought survives murder, enriched by it. Not only thought forms and thought seeds survive. So do attitudes, feeling dispositions. We have an enduring attraction to what survives death, to what survives murder. Somewhere in this *mélange* is a burning hope that we survive ourselves. Perhaps Socrates shows us this is possible, or at least whets our appetite for a brand of life that withstands us.

*   *   *

Questions of a spreading I arise. When I say I, I do not mean only my I, but all Is. All Is everywhere. I killed Socrates means all Is killed Socrates. And go on killing him. Something like being a universal Christ killer.

I am tempted to call the spreading I part of psycho-logic, mad logic, or, in an age of innocence, possibly a kind of baby logic, in a demonic age, demon logic. For convenience, I will stick with psycho-logic, or mad logic, and mean by it something boundless.

I am aware that boundless might be something spiritual and by using the notation mad or psycho I am putting a slant on what I wish to convey. This is correctable, but for now let us ride with the deformation.

A spreading I. In this case, my I spreading. A necessary conclusion I come to is that I am responsible for the death of every human being. I caused death. I brought death into the world. This may seem a rather extreme extension of universal guilt. But it is a clear and distinct idea, apodictic. Once conceived, it is self-evident.

There are many analogues. Oedipus's sin becomes a national sin. In the Bible, a house may fall ill as a result of sin and land may become ill as well. Sin spreads. Something rotten in the state of Denmark goes through the body politic, the social body. Sin often spreads from top to bottom, not, as is popularly conceived, from bottom up. The sins of royalty, governing and judicial bodies, owners of media, power nodes of society set the tone. Look what the Bush group did to the spirit of our age in service of rapacious boundlessness. Yes, predatory currents precede them, but they add their own wounding signature to soaring national guilt.

There is such a thing as denied or deferred guilt, displaced guilt. Leaders disown guilt for their atrocities and look elsewhere for guilty parties. They blame others for what they themselves have done or will do. They cultivate insensitivity to results of their actions and often succeed in feeling justified (a perverse use of the idea of justice). Denial of guilt spreads, too. Guilt and denial of guilt constitute a pairing, Siamese twins. As Bion (2005, p. 91) wrote in a related context, "They are not really separable, but one is the extreme of the other, as if they were polarized".

There is a psycho or mad dimension to thinking–feeling that is there at all times. And one way it works is *spreading boundlessness, boundless spread*. Deniers are not free of boundless spread. They smear others with the denied element or some substitution for it. One paints the world with feelings in semi-blind ways.

*   *   *

Here I am in the Garden of Eden once again. And what do I do? I bring death into the world. In this myth of beginnings, evil, sin, and death are attributed to human causality. Not to any human, but me and you. We did it. *I* am Adam, Eve, and serpent, and so are *you*. Here our Is are indistinguishable even though they have different profiles: variants of 1, *a plural 1*.

Our system spontaneously gravitates towards an I (mine, yours, someone else's) as a causal organizer. My fault, your fault, our fault. We try to fend off a sense of helplessness in face of forces we do not control. By claiming guilt or causal efficacy for terrifying facts like mortality, we try to control the uncontrollable and make terror go away. The possibility that we are guilty in relative ways spreads into absolutist thinking.

We have thought forms that tell us we can live forever if we are good enough and act in certain ways or have certain beliefs. We can undo death. We make death live and can make death die. This sounds like a crushing responsibility, part of boundless spread.

The fact that we create stories that tell us death is our fault tells us something about our minds in its I-centric aspect. The fact that all humanity shares blame does not get me off the hook. Guilt causality spreads both ways, individual ↔ group. I brought death into the world, but so did you. I as multiple: death owes its life to *us*. There is a social context to the link between causality and death. Adam, Eve, and the serpent all conspire, all play a role. Freud tells us that different parts of a dream are parts of the I. A bit of profound wisdom, but is it the whole truth?

Surely, the universe sends messages in dreams. I is not the only character. Life is an important character, life expressing itself about life and creating life, including dream life. Did I cause dreaming, or did life processes bring both dream and myself into existence, with or without my help?

The dream of the Garden of Eden overcomes us. A message it sends is that deep down we feel we caused death. The spreading I spreads guilt via a causal nexus, imaginary or real. The dream of

Eden tells us that we use guilt as an emotional organizer, an inner organizing principle similar to Kant's time, space, and causality. Guilt as a basic organizer of experience.

We try to rid ourselves of guilt and stain. Cleanse ourselves, clean up our act. But what needs to be cleaned cannot be wiped out of our nature. We may wipe ourselves out instead.

*   *   *

As I meditate on boundless guilt, a reversal begins. The syllogism, after all, says, "All men are mortal". I previously took it as meaning "If all men are mortal and Socrates is a man, then Socrates is mortal." If . . . a matter not settled.

But what if indeed all men *are* mortal? No ifs, ands, or buts. We all die and fear what much evidence points to, that death is final. No life for me after death. I do not have to reach a definitive conclusion in order for the syllogism to carry me along on this alternate, seemingly more objective path. All men are mortal.

Let us take this, for the moment, as an objective statement, a statement of what is, things as they are. The straightforward objectivity of such a statement frees me from my burden of guilt over the fact of death. For, if all men are mortal and that's just the way things are, a fact of life, there is the distinct possibility, even likelihood, that I am not the sole or main or even co-creator of death. Death has nothing at all to do with what I do or will. It just is. I am part of a life system in which death is.

What a relief!

*   *   *

As is often the case, a double attitude exists. It is not so easy to believe in death and not so easy not to. On the one hand, subjective spread; on the other, objective discrimination. The former tends towards boundlessness, the latter towards limits. In terms of I-sensation, boundless I and circumscribed I. In terms of guilt linked to causality, I caused it, you caused it: some I is to blame and maybe all Is.

A variant: *we* did it; no, it happens. It is natural; no, it can be superseded.

Death has a way of insinuating itself into beginnings. Two trees in the garden loom with special significance, life and knowledge, ubiquitous doubleness, as if they are separable. After the first couple ate of the tree of knowledge and knew good and evil, God makes haste to get them out of the garden before they eat of the tree of life and live forever. Conundrum: why on earth didn't He take the precaution to seal or hide the tree of life earlier? Is it that Adam and Eve would not think of eating from it because it was not forbidden? Wouldn't a tree of life exert special attraction? Or is it that eating from the tree of knowledge opens death, sin as death and literal death. And, with death anxiety, one seeks life eternal.

In the centre of the garden looms death, awaiting discovery in life's pulse. A spiritual Punch and Judy show. You know the bad thing is going to happen, only you do not know when. The garden narrative makes you feel it could have been otherwise *and* makes you feel it could not. It makes you feel there is something in the middle of this wondrous place that causes pain, something that does not have to be there but *is* there *and* has to be there.

It would be jejune to say the cause of pain is the tangle of attitudes the story portrays: comminglings of permissions–prohibitions, interest, curiosity, envy, pride, titillation, yearning, hunger, hope, desire: affective attitudes all mixed up. Garden as cauldron of seething excitations, expectations, attitudes. The narrative puts tracers on tendencies and tries to disentangle some of them.

God created the universe and its parts and said repeatedly, "It is good." Adam and Eve ate of its parts and saw evil as well as good. Did they see more than God? Experience more? Was God protecting them from seeing too much too soon, more than was good for them? Was God protecting them from feeling ashamed?

Wise people say Adam and Eve had incomplete views. To see life as evil is short-sighted. God does all for the good of our souls. Were Adam and Eve like children who call something bad because it pains them? They disobeyed God and felt shame. Going against God's wishes pained them? Individuality pained them? Difference pained them? God gave them a chance to be ashamed.

We do not know what evil they knew. They saw something they did not see before or entered a way of seeing previously unavailable. Evil emerges as something new. A form of knowledge, a new form of knowledge. A direct knowing, direct seeing. They saw something: evil itself. And it was not separable from themselves: psychic as well as physical nakedness.

The psychic load we carry quickly gets to be too much. The emergence of psychic being, wondrous as it is, is more than we can bear. Coming into life takes us deep into the impossible. And all that is possible seems delicate and immense.

Where is the garden now? The kingdom of heaven is in us. Where inside us? Through the centre of the pain.

To be gardeners is a gentle beginning. Yet, I sense Hamlet's presence breathing in the wings. An agitated breathing. Hamlet in the Garden? I look more closely. I glimpse his form standing with his hands on two trees, one on life, one knowledge, like Samson, awaiting a moment of strength. A strength made not of knowing or physical might, but of piercing perception. He does not speak yet, not much, but words are gathering. They will pour out of an invisible serpent's bite that does not heal. The same serpent that roamed the garden before Adam and Eve, making waves, looking for company.

The same serpent that made time go faster by dreaming Hamlet as an imaginary companion. Adam and Eve, actual people, came as quite a disappointment. Until he realized that they were part of a story, too.

* * *

In an interview, Ingmar Bergmann said he did not believe in guilt. He felt that guilt distracts one from the real pain one causes others, the real suffering one inflicts.

One quickly imagines he is also speaking of his own suffering. If the centre of one's being suffers, it is difficult not to communicate this to others. We are permeable. Feelings spread.

But he means more. His behaviour towards a son was gratuitously cruel, as if his son became a special pocket for cruelty to lodge. Nothing a son in one's charge deserves. Bergmann says he was a bad father and communicates inevitability, given his own nature. He is unapologetic. It is part of the mystery of who he is, something that happens, partly connected with pain from his own childhood and his own parents. Suffering whose beginnings cannot be exhausted.

Does he take responsibility for something he cannot help? Does he take responsibility for who he is? He neither owns nor disowns it. He lives it, what part he can live. Cruelty as part of the mystery of being. His form of witness is to turn cruelty into profound art, sharing inevitable suffering on the screen. His movies bear witness to suffering existence. They show, not explain. They share inmost pain many of us instantaneously recognize. It is as if he can do no more. This kind of showing is precisely the sharing he *can* do. For this, we are grateful.

*   *   *

A person who consults me comes in. I am eating a pear. We look at each other and I become conscious that I am destroying the tissues of the pear. The pear is a living thing. Not animate like you or I, perhaps. But real enough with life of its own, which I am killing.

I tell the person I am with (let's call her Sea, by which I also mean see) that I am a murderer and she is watching me destroy life. We kill to live, there is no way around it, even if we are vegetarians. She is witnessing a murder. I go on detailing the ripping of the tissues of the pear with my teeth, the chewing, swallowing. It is a slow, juicy destruction. I well understand hunger strikes, anorexia, the refusal to kill, the refusal to live at the expense of others.

I can do what a certain religious impulse suggests: thank the pear for its self-giving, honour its precious contribution to my well being. I may even convince myself the pear is participating in a willing sacrifice through which it sanctifies itself. I get to an uneatable part of the rind and stem, all that's left of its visible form. The main part of its holiness is now inside me.

Sea is distraught, possibly teary, or perhaps I am misreading her. I do feel something though, something intense, compact, positive. As if a dense radioactive pellet of self inside Sea shines, a new discovery, a new self-feeling of a sort. She draws herself close around a small, dark strength. I could be wrong. It all takes places very quickly, these micro-perceptions. What is most wondrous in this work is most elusive, scarcely felt perturbations in a darkish background.

Sea deals with chronic psychic overload. She discovered her father's hanging body when she was a child. Her mother's next husband, a good man whom Sea loved, was mutilated by work machinery in her middle childhood. Her mother's third husband, cold and mean, survived.

Sea survived many therapies and was a prescient mental health worker herself. She was lucky to find work that her trauma world fit. By helping others, she spent her life helping herself. Going through this ghastly bit of history was nothing new. Why was it in the room now? What was it asking this afternoon?

She grew up with farm animals, but could not get used to their slaughter. Images of slit throats and beheaded creatures subliminally tortured her. She developed a fear of going near certain animals, a fear she tried to hide. No one would understand. They would make fun of her, play it down, question its basis, make it unreal. What, after all, could they do with dread? An incommunicable stream of death ran through childhood and permeated her aloneness. She could not express it to herself or others in ways that made "acceptable" sense. Where does horror with no place go?

I was listening carefully, feeling carefully. Therapy as home for horror. Some people need to be in therapy all their lives as it is the only place their horror is comfortable.

I share an image: "You must have felt through your childhood like a chicken with its head cut off." I meant to convey what her feelings felt like. Running amok, headless, separated, severed. A head that refuses to die, a body that does not die. They go through the years together, mutilated, nerves twitching, nameless, placeless, disorientated. A brutal stream of death keeps one's being on edge.

Sea responds immediately. For the moment the image fits. I will not say it exactly brings relief, but something like relief: contact with the unsayable, a point of contact with herself. Not that that image had always been there, but something reverberates, a sensed truth about one's condition. It is not for nothing phrases like this are a common part of language. They express and track states we tend not to know what to do with. So often, perhaps all we can do is note that they exist. To do more takes away from them, mars them. They so much want respect from us and need caring regard. Odd to say about something so internal: they want us to let them in, at least a bit, a bit more. They want us to let our insides in.

*   *   *

Socrates spoke of a chicken when he was dying, a debt he owed. He instructed his students to tell his wife to return a chicken to the rightful party.

Socrates' death, as narrated by Plato, must rank as one of the great deaths of all time. He did not leave as a chicken without a head. To meet death as he did, to not be chicken (again, vernacular instructs us about our states), constitutes more than a model. It is a tribute to life.

*   *   *

To temporarily conclude this little reverie, I would like to say a few words about three forms that guilt can take: (1) functional; (2) mystic; (3) transcendent. The names are a bit arbitrary, but not entirely.

1. *Function.* Guilt, along with shame and fear, plays an important role in regulating social relations. It functions as a kind of warning when going too far in one or another direction. It tells one to draw back and reassess the situation. It is part of social sensing, a kind of inner compass that says, go this way, that way, too much, too little. It helps contain and regulate injury.

A kind of *wheelbarrow model* (an image I believe I read in Solomon Asch, *Social Psychology*) is relevant here. Picture two people having to move a load in a wheelbarrow from here to there, across ruts and between obstacles, each person gripping one arm of the barrow. A lot of spontaneous, implicit, mutual sensing must go on to keep the barrow upright and on the way. You might say guilt, shame, and fear play such a role in social relations. They are part of inner sensing, related to our own aloneness and responsibility, and, at the same time, part of the tissue of living experience with others.

It is a sensing that applies to being with oneself, living with oneself. Shall I do this, that, be this that, go this way, that way. It touches what kind of person I wish to be, or can be, or am. It helps to set direction, to chart a course.

Similarly, it is part of the self-corrective movement of social activity from family to nation, including world relations. For there is—or should be—something that can be called national guilt, shame, fear (the last often part of prudence).

Guilt, shame, and fear *might* lead to self-reflection, corrective vision, and remodelling of one's picture of life, including reassessments of the contexts in which one exists.

2. *Mystic*. Guilt, on occasion, propels one to places not normally reached by functional guilt embedded in co-operative, affiliative behaviour. Mystical guilt tends to be more intensely individual. Its personal intensity leads to a radically transformational experience of one's own psychic space. Although functional guilt is part of its background, mystical guilt can lead to such radical self-questioning that the structure of social existence and life itself is placed in doubt, interrogated, found guilty.

Although many inner or outer circumstances can trigger it, mystic guilt is often propelled by excruciating realization of one's own destructiveness and agony over the fact that destructiveness is built into life.

One would like to be a life form that does not cause pain and one's heart cries out, "Why, God, did you make me this way, one who must kill to live?" Or merely, one who must injure to live. For no one avoids injuring others or oneself. Anorexia or other forms of potential and actual suicide become understandable in terms of the wish not to be a killer. Anorexia as critical protest against, and refusal in face of, the way life is structured: one must destroy even to eat. Anorexia as moral critique of existence.

There is mystical guilt that can border on certain forms of psycho-spiritual anorexia. Fasts of the spirit, as well as physical fasts. Nevertheless, no amount of self-purging can eliminate the propensity to injure or be injured by one's own or another's intentions, bearing, cruelty, acts. We may try to protect others from ourselves or ourselves from others and possibly succeed in diminishing the sum of injury. But we will never be destruction free.

However, the fact that we will not succeed in ever becoming the kind of persons we would like to be does not free us from facing this defeat. A dangerous sense of defeat runs through our nature. It may never be totally exhumed but it must be met. That is, we must meet our inner defeat as part of meeting ourselves, part of our life-long introduction to ourselves.

Unmet inner defeat tends to exacerbate hidden areas of collapse that suck at our beings. The collapse may not be totally correctable, but it makes a difference if we try to sense it and get on working terms with it. To discover enduring areas of collapse is one thing, to collapse into collapse another.

To kill ourselves because we are killers, to starve ourselves out of existence, is a cop-out. It not only collapses collapse, it evades basic facts of our existence. We must sustain our sense of collapse as part of the working materials we are given. We are challenged to develop new relationships to unpleasant facts of our makeup.

Mystical guilt evolves, partly, as a refusal to collapse in face of guilt or in face of all we have to be guilty about. It does not give in to artificial soft-soaping, cheap I'm OK, You're OK forms of Job's comforters. We have come upon a kind of inverse Job, a Job who feels guilty for the way life works, its appalling mercilessness, its inherent destructiveness. Not a Job who claims innocence, but who embraces the full pain of existence in his very core. A Job who, far from being righteous, cannot escape a basic flaw and opens the array of difficulties that being a wounding–wounded being entails. A Job who sustains the maximum punch that guilt can deliver.

The new Job refuses or is unable to collapse any part of guilt, mediating a kind of cosmic guilt, life's guilt over its own nature. Life guilty for itself, channelled in one's own person. One cannot blame life for being what it is and sidestep being a fact of life oneself. One may be tempted to get out of life by ending one's own, but that leads nowhere. An apple (rotten? poisoned? juicy?) bites into us and keeps on biting. We may not be able to stop life's bite, but refusal to make believe what is happening is not happening opens new spaces. We change by our immense effort to confront what cannot be solved.

I sometimes describe this as a kind of psychic wormhole. We keep batting our heads against walls and something in our psyche opens, takes us somewhere that did not exist a moment before. We go in one place, come out another. A new portion of being is exposed or created. We feel differently because we are in another portion of existence.

There are stories that talk about a hole in the ground or going through a mirror or magical furniture, a wardrobe, a carpet, some point of entry to somewhere else, another existential plane. We play down this experience by calling it fantasy. Or overplay it by solidifying it into institutional religion. Or turn it into a sideshow or con by pointing to fakirs who exploit it.

What I am trying to point to is something intensely personal. As if the psyche is perforated by its own intensity and one finds oneself in another part of vast, unknown terrain without discernible forms or objects, just hints, ineffable sensings, something not liquid or solid or gaseous, yet mysteriously existing, an elusive landscape or background painted with tones of light and dark.

One finds oneself far away from the immovable wall one failed to penetrate. One day soon, one might bump into that or another wall and head-banging will resume. But, for the moment, one is somewhere else, another place. One failed to penetrate the wall but somehow penetrated oneself. Something in the core of one's being gave way. And, like stories where one is whisked away by an unknown force, one is whisked to another state of being.

It may take years, much of a lifetime, to catch up with the discovery of such a little known or used capacity. But each time one tastes it, one feels the possibility of peace beyond understanding, bliss, happiness. One feels the thing itself. A discovery that stays fresh with use: one can never get enough of it. It adds a moving glow to existence, good or bad. One tries to channel, dose, and map it and, in some significant, if tiny ways, succeeds. But it is gracious enough, kind enough, to remain unmappable.

How could one know when one started that guilt was one of the privileged lines through which to reach it? But perhaps we might say any way that mediates this contact is privileged.

A hallmark of mystic guilt is the immense desire one conceives to cause harm no more. It is a desire that perforates one's inmost soul and, while it motivates self-struggle and the need to be a better person, it also, mysteriously, takes us to a freer place. It relates to a love described biblically as loving God with all your heart, mind, might, and soul. It mobilizes all one is and can be as a gift of love.

3. *Transcendent.* Mystic guilt begins in pain and torment over injury one causes and leads to intense, persistent self-wrestling in determination to become a better person. A side-effect is the amazing discovery of psycho-spiritual domains one did not know existed, a kind of amazing grace. One does not stop wanting or trying to be a better person. But the struggle is now touched with more mercy and compassion, which take the edge off of severity.

Thomas Merton somewhere wrote, "The secret of our identity is in God's mercy". The discovery of the mercy that pervades the psycho-spiritual universe is life changing, softening. It does not stop the pain or torment of guilt. One still fails in one's care and service, one's wish to help rather than harm. One still chokes on inescapable shortcomings, the bad apple one is. But the good one participates in uplifts life, offers purpose.

There is, however, a further step that transcends the torments of guilt with its goodness and badness and the depths of honest struggle. My first taste of it happened in a puff, a nanosecond. Something I read in a Buddhist text, which I have not been able to locate, and in less than a micro-instant, something was added and has evolved. "Added" is not quite right for this sudden, life-changing, self-changing happening. In that moment, guilt vanished. Another taste of being occurred. I cannot exactly call it guiltless, since, as time continued, I realized that motivating guilt still existed as a subtext in another region of being, important and life informing. But not the last word.

To be true to the new experience, I must say that I felt free of guilt. In a pop it was gone. I could scarcely believe it and looked around for it. Stretching into the new world, I could breathe more easily. My limbs felt lighter. Oppression I had not quite fully recognized lifted.

I tested the new happening by calling up bad things I did that chronically tortured me. I could see some of them working in their domains, but they were dimmer. They did not have the same impact, the punch they used to have. The bite was gone.

At first, I was afraid to smile. I was afraid relief would vanish or be taken away if I pushed too hard. I dared not take the new space for granted and make too big a step. It may sound strange that something so freeing made me so uptight, afraid to move and spoil it. Something that allowed me to breathe freely made me afraid to breathe.

But I breathed anyway, looked around, tasted, and smelled. I could not believe my good luck. It was true. The guilt fell away, or took less space, or became less important, more a faint imprint than a crushing bulldozer, if there at all.

It was as if I had been a different person when I did the things that haunted me. A lower, other me, a me I could not help being when I did the bad things that never let go. In less than a flash, that being was superseded. I entered a new plane of being and what occurred in "lower" regions became less haunting, less relevant, lost meaning.

Now, the truth is, nothing goes away and terms like lower and higher are misleading. But the unexpected is added or, better than added, changes the distribution of all that makes one up. Changes the way life feels, the way life *is*. In an experiential instant, a new capacity emerged and I would have to get to know myself all over again. I would have to test it as well as relish it. I would have to learn about its terrain. I would have to let it teach me.

The unexpected can be traumatic or releasing. Experience teaches me that adult traumas can be worse than childhood traumas. No time of life has a monopoly on pain and injury. I have seen adults die in the wake of trauma that a child could weather.

At times, release comes, and you see what might lead people to feel "saved", liberated from life's oppressive elements. In ordinary parlance, to be saved means to be saved from danger or a bad situation, as in to save a life. The word also means "savings", money or goods one has accumulated that make one feel safer and freer materially. But it also applies to soul, to save one's soul from grave or mortal danger, from sin and evil and its own self-oppression.

In the instant I am trying to touch, oppression fell away and I felt a fresh freedom that made my being smile. Everything that tormented me was gone. As religions say, I was another being. Not quite, of course, since I am still me being another being, with a welcome difference.

A story of the Buddha comes to mind. In telling it, I am taking liberties, telling it my way, my inner Buddha, so I hope you will make allowances. There are walls one pits oneself against which, for some of us, become a matter of life and death. For Siddartha Gautama, the fact of suffering was such a wall. Suffering built into life, what people to do themselves, to each other, disasters of many kinds, natural and man made, sickness, evil, death, life's cruelty, self's cruelty. The Buddha sat with this unforgiving fact. Unbudgeable fact *vs.* unbudgeable sitter. He could not stop life from being injurious. He could not make death go away. But, in sitting with unyielding facts, parts of a great wall, something happens. The wall does not go away. Something inside changes.

One throws oneself against the unmovable with all one's being and being opens. One cannot change the fact of living and dying, but one can change one's approach to it. One can become a different kind of avenue to the inevitable and unexpected. Students might ask him questions about life after death, or other imponderables. He would try to refocus things back to the change of being he discovered. "I can't answer all the questions you ask," Buddha might say. "They're outside the boundaries of my discovery. Oh, I can recite establishment beliefs about whether or not death is final. But that's not my domain of expertise. I'm a specialist in one main thing, the fact of suffering. And I'm sharing with you a way of approaching it."

Even a taste of this change in being goes a long way, although hunger shouts for more.

CHAPTER SIX

Revenge ethics

Hamlet is asked to avenge his father's murder. He hesitates somewhat, not a very long time. It seems so long because of everything that goes on inside him. Shakespeare creates a sense of inner monologue that runs throughout the dialogues of the play. It is psychic time that seems so long, an underlying counterpoint to external events and linear time, the march of history. The play is drenched in subjective depths that seem to last forever.

In *Rage* (2001b), I wrote that Hamlet did not hesitate enough. He was caught between alternative "ethics", primitive blood revenge and an ethics of subjectivity. I think all revenge is blood revenge. One feels bloodied and responds in kind. Eye for eye, tooth for tooth. Yet, more is involved than equalizing pain. Revenge takes place in an aura of magnification. Pain and blood and wounds and rage are acutely magnified. Literature and cinema portray vengeful faces as distorted. One's being undergoes deformations, visible and invisible.

An inner meaning of revenge ethics is: one tries to right things, redress an injury, right a wrong. Revenge is on the side of some kind of sense of justice, an affective attitude that has pervaded much religion. The just God seeks revenge for sin, correcting what has gone awry. A distillation of this tendency is God's urge to wipe out sinful humanity, blotting out disturbance by annihilating it. The image of a primordial flood has never left. Freud called flooding a primal trauma and emotional storms of infancy, in one form or another, find expression, even gather momentum, all life long (Eigen, 2005).

One of the most dramatic, yet common, floods connected to revenge is rage. Rage is one of the most total experiences many have, and one of the most traumatizing. Its ingredients include mixes of orgasmic destruction, injury, plea, judgement, and vindication.

To wipe out pain and disturbance, to wipe out disturbing others with the effects of fury, seems almost reasonable for a moment to the rager. He feels justified, and in the flash of rage, a bit god-like. God's primal urge to blot out disturbance becomes something of a "tropism" in the psyche, giving the subject a god-ish thrill. To be inflamed by rage, blinded, is to share the taste of fury of a wounded, vengeful god.

Note, in passing, an anal reference in the use of annihilation to fight feeling annihilated, to blot out, wipe out, wipe trouble off the face of the earth, clean life up. To be pure by wiping out anality: a mad unconscious vision of an asshole-free existence to be achieved by soiling and spoiling. One reverses being shit on by wiping the filthy smile off the other's face. Rage and revenge as cleansing agents, psychic shit as cleanser.

There is a heart-smile inside that we protect, feel paranoid about. A precious smile inside we are afraid to show. We turn into attack dogs to guard it. We fear toxins seeping into it, spoiling it forever, ruining a basic sense of self. Rage channelled through revenge is one way to feel whole and pure again, an attempt to rid ourselves of heart toxins by a violent sense of right, a purity pump that can be fatal.

Revenge stretches over time. The rage that it contains can be filtered though long-term calculation, perverse patience. A lot of planning went into destroying the World Trade Center. The bombers were assured that disturbances in their life would be gone. They would actualize a disturbance-free state by righting insidious wrongs, wounding a source of injury. Part of the genius of suicide bombing—beyond political logistics—is the extraordinary gratification involved by fusing all-out devotion with all-out destruction. Two basic tendencies, to devote and to destroy, achieve, for a time, maximum merger.

Bush's rush to war with Iraq uses ingredients shared by our attackers. It plays on the sense of being wronged, the need to right things, to blot out disturbance. These blend with a feeling of patriotic wholeness, a kind of obliterating wholeness, since counter-thoughts and contrary data are degraded, if not wiped out. A powerful lust for revenge is channelled by the calculations of power structures, mixing corporate interests with military, political, and religious spectacle. We do not use suicide bombers or cut heads off innocent civilians. But, in a profound sense, every solider who died in Iraq was on a suicide mission. Blood lust is an underside of the will to power. There is no such thing as "clean" power where human lives are involved.

Rage-revenge is almost always an act of self-affirmation at another's expense. Depending on context, there is something positive, a need to be heard, to energize one's existence, to find a path to effectiveness and importance, to have an impact. We are out to affirm ourselves, but have not discovered how to do this without vast negative expense. Something tyrannical is part of psycho-social structures, part of self-affirmation.

There is also strong desire not to be tyrannical if one can help it, to rein in the tyranny thread, to care. Hamlet gave in to tyranny but made great discoveries on the way. Had he not succumbed to a revenge ethics, he might have valorized an ethics of subjectivity. The true hero of the play, after all, is the human subject, the stream of thoughts and feelings Hamlet had, Hamlet's free associations, reveries, obsessions. Shakespeare opens a subjective world and the ostensible protagonist falls through many dimensions of it.

Freud's abstinence rule ("absent thyself from felicity awhile") is designed to allow us not to take sides, not to decide: a vacation from decision making in order to glimpse other psychic fields. As we contact more than we knew or thought we were, and allow a larger psychic field to contact us, we discover and validate a certain value to waiting, staying open, an ethics of indecision.

Hamlet was not Hamlet enough. He succumbed too readily to the blood ethic, but he gives us hints of something else, the drama of subjectivity with its quandary of being adrift in multi-dimensionality, hungering for many worlds at once, drenched with many worlds at once. Uncertainty, not knowing, wavering, wondering, the taste of experiencing as such. To be adrift, to sense unconscious processes working: a different kind of patience than plotting for a chance to get even or assert power. In radical contrast to much that is valued in normative politics, where weakness (sensitivity, feelings, many-sidedness) is ridiculed and show of strength is overrated. The flaw Hamlet is most criticized for-vacillation—is a portal to a world of subjective sensitivity very much needed.

An ethics of sensitivity, sensitive awareness to the precious subjective life of every human being (Eigen, 2004). A politician who was asked how he felt about losing an election said, "I severed my nerve endings long ago or I couldn't survive in politics." It is horrible to think how many of our leaders may share this "necessary" dread of feeling, a nation of severed sensitivity.

There is another kind of right than the right of revenge. A desire to do right by ourselves and others, to do justice to life, the struggle to become partners with our capacities rather than be controlled by a model of control. Feelings do matter. There cannot be truth without them. There are people who care what happens to people.

Power politics tells us to hide the fact that we are sensitive beings. Sensitivity is for sissies. But we *are* sensitive beings touched by what we do to others, as well as what others do to us. We remain empty if we cannot give.

Soldiers discover that the sense of being "right" does not save them from deforming effects of killing. The trauma of being a murderer scars sensitivity, damage one never stops recovering from. Even if murder is justified, the soul is scarred. Psychopaths are able to live with a great deal of scar tissue, perhaps know little else. It is not unusual to go about one's business, looking the other way from the harm one does to others. But the pain is felt by many.

An ethics of sensitivity, with care for weakness, vacillation, indecision, unknowing—which is to say, a kind of sensitive openness—does not seem to have much of a chance in this profit-driven world. But I am not willing to count it out. There is a still, small voice in the margins, an evolution that awaits us.

CHAPTER SEVEN

Something wrong

D r Z: "Sex is not desire so much as needing to feel OK. I don't mean the push and drive of sex and then relief and discharge. I mean the sense of something wrong. A sense of something wrong with me and sex makes me feel OK.

"Sex makes me feel OK as a person, in my core. Something wrong in my core for some moments gets washed clean by sex. A kind of baptism, cleansing, resetting of self.

"Sex makes people feel dirty *and* clean. There is a history of sex as sullying, corrupting. Sex as sin, associated with the wretched, dying, decaying body. Something associated with shame, guilt, fear. Sex as menace, disruption, cruel. Something bad.

"Sex makes people feel happy, light, caring, warm, triumphant, fulfilled, justified. A more intense version of what can happen when people say hello to each other, exchange greetings, smiles, inquiries."

* * *

Grace: "Desire is cosmic. Sex opens me. Fear is part of it. You swim in light, fear, hope, God. I want the other person to be happy and that is important. But that is part of what happens along the way. You leave the other behind and something else opens up. Something that life hides and promises and then it's there. And the good that is there makes the thing that feels wrong go away."

*   *   *

Dr Z: "How can I not be in pain? We don't care for the environment that supports life and care even less for the emotional environment that supports persons. Pain for my patients who seek help from someone so inept and inadequate. Pain for my children because my joy in them is so deep.

"You can't take my pain away, and I wouldn't want you to. You're in the same boat, another person who happens to be a therapist. Two therapists in the room together, except *I* happen to be going to *you*.

"I read your description of a hallucinatory shield, a lie barrier, a bubble that makes our world psychologically soundproof. You wrote about hallucinating yourself as not there. How else is it possible to be led into a lying war, unless hallucinating oneself not there?

"No one in this day and age should be surprised that people vote against their own interests. If psychoanalysis shows anything, it's a self-sabotaging streak in our nature. It works on a smaller scale with individuals, a larger scale in nations. Financial greed and madness of empire, Trojan horses our nature smuggles into society for its self-destruction.

"A lie bubble immunizes the very rich against the cries of the world. The same bubble makes the rest of us feel we have no impact. But we imagine having an impact and imaginings fester.

"Telling my patients what they are doing to hurt themselves doesn't help. Information isn't enough. We are made of layers of adaptations capped by a pretence of rationality. Most of our show of rationality is make-believe rationality. Our adaptations are filled with pretence too. We are filled with layers of sedimented pretence. Rationality compounds the pain. Our earnestness and urgency are irrelevant against cumulative feints, reshufflings, deformations, twists.

"What can you say to make an impact when your I undergoes a warp? Some absorb something new better than others. We guard our deformations. Bubbles grow around them. And around our lives.

"I'm thinking of a likeable woman who does not have friends. She is likeable in theory. Pleasant looks, personality, interests. Yet she is somehow out of play, inured. There's a bubble around her others feel.

"Yes, she's attractive, appealing, yet she slides off you. It's not that she doesn't want to be with you. She does. But she is not with you. She is *unable* to be with you. She is somewhere else or nowhere. Looks good, sounds good, tastes good, but when you go towards her you slide off. You cannot reach her. You reach a bubble.

"Her marriage is falling apart. She blames her husband—*all* his fault. Not that he is not at fault, but *all*? She deflects blame. Like Adam and Eve, *It's not my fault*. It's someone else's or no one's. To deflect responsibility goes beyond blame. Responsibility isn't a matter of blame or guilt or cause, it's to put more of oneself into one's life, respond to life more fully. It's as if she deflects herself away from herself out of fear of glimpsing an obscure and undetected psychic defect.

"Here in her marriage there's a clue to the bubble. In her marriage the bubble is blown up and ugly. With friends it does not reach this level of intensity. The bubble contains a negative hallucination of sorts. It hallucinates an incapacity away. It erases a failure to let in an inability to admit wrong. The result of this negative hallucination, this bubble, is that she cannot and does not know that she is unable to admit ever being wrong. Not wrong about this or that little thing, but existential wrong, wrong about being, *her* being or another's being. She cannot feel in any meaningful and reaching way that she is wrong about the nature of things, the way she lives, who she is, or estimations about the who and what of others, or that others can really be right about *her*.

"How is it possible that being wrong eludes her? Is it an inborn defect, an equipment shortage? I don't think so. I think it is a chronic response to chronic trauma. A way of shielding herself from what was horrible in childhood and what continues to be horrible inside her. From an early age she knew others were in the wrong. Her father had sex with her and she kept quiet about it. Now she never stops accusing and blaming the wrong persons for the wrong things. A shield of accusation stops her from growing. A blame bubble stops her from touching her own insides.

"Sexual abuse was something she could point to but there were other things harder to point to. Abuse covered emotional warp and deprivation that left her feeling impoverished, twisted. Filled with inner waste lands she could not go near, covered over by the twins, defiance and collapse: "It's not my fault."

"She needs relationships, support. I can't tell her she's halluci-nating a blameless state. Blameless she may be at bottom, but it is a paralysing attitude. Something in her keeps asserting an existen-tial blamelessness that makes her inaccessible. It's as if the sense of being blameless has become part of the disease, a kind of protective shield that stops her from feeling more of herself. Blamelessness stops her from feeling devastation. It's not whether or not she is to blame. It's that an attitude of blamelessness keeps her sealed off from letting others in. Others fall off a basic inaccessibility that she does not perceive.

"I feel this blameless inaccessibility as a hallucinatory force. She wouldn't get it. It's too scary, perhaps not even right. Perhaps it's more a subtle interaction between perception and projection. She does not let in whole areas of inner perception. She cannot bear much negative about herself. Her perception is tied up with project-ing negativity. She *sees* others as doing something bad to her. She *sees* badness as happening out there and, God knows, enough is. Yet I sense an invisibly toxic hallucination she has no way to detect. Am I hallucinating it? Perhaps a way to know someone else's halluci-nation is to hallucinate it yourself. Quiet, lifelong hallucinations with lasting effects, histories of wounds wrapped in hallucinatory bubbles.

"She is filled with self-generated ideas that slide off people. She is like a child who cannot locate what is painful because the pain is too much and radiates far from the source. She grows as best she can around incapacity to deal with pain, incapacity that translates into questions like, "Why don't I have more friends? Why aren't my kids better? Why is the world like this?"

"Deep down, mostly unconscious, sometimes with searing consciousness, is the secret sense that what is painful is that there is something wrong with me, something horribly wrong, worthless, unlovable. That may be the core of the bubble, part of the core. And the more she is in that place, the less access there is for conversation, for contact.

"I'm like a submarine with a periscope and sonar, locating in my patient a sense of something wrong. A sense not limited to this woman. There is something wrong not only with this or that personality. It spreads throughout a community, shared by the international community, a world state. There are many explanations for it. But nothing erases it.

"I am not exempting myself, or you. I know there are ways I am inaccessible and I have no doubt you are, too. What I am more afraid of are ways we are out of reach that we have no idea about at all."

*   *   *

Grace: "It's not just that they make you feel wrong but that you are *The Wrong*. An avatar of *The Wrong*. As far back as I remember I was *The Wrong*. And part of the feeling is the sense that I am their *Wrong*. Wrong for them, wrong for everyone. As a little girl, I searched for someone who didn't see me as The Wrong, someone for whom I mattered. I almost found it in teachers, but not quite.

"My hospitalizations started in my teens. Maybe in hospitals the good would happen. If it did, it did not get through to me. I was an uncorrectable imprint of The Wrong. And I saw The Wrong in grown-ups who were trying to help me. I had a sick sense that even helpers made me a special conduit of the wrong they breathed, a taint no one could bear. The Wrong swallowed up the world.

"Inquisitors torture you into realizing you are The Wrong, then leave you. They stick The Wrong into you and do not need you until the next surge. The Wrong is like a sex urge in them that builds, climaxes, then leaves for a while. When it builds, they need me to put it into.

"Underneath a face is another face, a knife that lives in blood and pain. A famished knife. Does it take a psychotic to see insides of humans as hungry knives?

"I turned to Jesus with total intensity when I was a little girl. Someone who got it, who knew The Wrong, the pain, and triumphed over it. Jesus, a lightning rod for The Wrong of this world.

"My mind is a mist. Was Jesus the more of life? Did he triumph over life? A greater life? The fall back to myself was always hard.

Back on earth there was just me. Jesus did not clean The Wrong out of me. I was still unclean me. The Wrong is part of my essence, part of the pulse of life.

"There are moments of joy in which one transcends The Wrong. The Wrong is eclipsed by joy. One appreciates such moments, but The Wrong comes back with a wallop.

"I hear the words of the psalm, "I am poor and destitute, my heart has died within me". This feels like something right. It is not that I am dead when I feel these words. No, it's as if The Wrong dies while these words live. As if The Wrong is the cross of this world and there are, for moments, saving words. Soul words that live, a kind of life that cancels The Wrong. While I am alive in these words The Wrong does not win. The one is a trauma I will never recover from, the other a death that passes into life.

"Was there ever a time before Something Wrong? I don't think so.

"There was something wrong in the Garden of Eden. A snake telling lies, tempting stories with links to destruction. Our lives are stories, God's stories I used to think. I still feel God very close to us, closer than ever. Sometimes I am ashamed for not hating God more.

"We are the garden, the liars, the story-telling snakes. The sea, the air, the animals, the flowers compacted in us. We *are* destructive creativity. As God is.

"Garden of Eden, garden of evil. Some people *really* lie and pass real lies off as truth. Like making up a God story and saying it really happened when it is really a literary event, a spiritual event. We tell stories about a destructive urge in the garden of life. Are we afraid to say that we like this destructive urge? That this urge is a way into life?

"Is this secret? The garden gives birth to destruction, *is* destructive birthing, nourishes destruction. Inside the nursing infant and caring mother do I see snakes? When does belief become destructive—madness of religions, imagining destruction-free life as they destroy.

"We imagine being expelled from the Garden because we need to imagine a place that is destruction free. A place to look back at or forward to. We look away from the fact that destruction was already in the garden, waiting for us as part of us.

"The garden tells us it feels good to be alive, but destruction comes. We are appalled at the need to destroy and draw back and double in on ourselves, and try to think beyond destruction, think of ways to outwit destruction, ways to use destruction to some day return to a destruction-free place or create one. A place we can only imagine.

"And what is real? Making believe destruction doesn't exist, pretending to be masters of destruction, hiding, doing what we can."

*   *   *

Dr Z: "Chimpanzees pick ticks and gnats off each other's fur and skin. We pick lies off each other's insides. Different ways of cleaning.

"It's hard to see our own lies. They meld into beliefs. We believe something strongly and excuse the lying part of it. A public figure said that Ariel Sharon's stroke was a punishment for dividing the Holy Land. You can't prove he's wrong, can you? It's his belief. Is it only belief? What can you say about retribution thinking? It's pretty strong and prevalent. It almost seems natural. If something bad happens, it's a punishment. If something good happens, it's a reward.

"Beliefs can take you to pretty strange places, blood-curdling places. Beliefs can take you to war and almost sound ethical. Beliefs can trap you into closing doors on yourself and stop you from hearing what is wrong.

"Hospitality to listening. Is anyone outside this invitation? There's a thinning out of attention, of caring. The media shrinks things. Ideas get thinner, feelings get nastier. Is the will to win thinning life out? *We must win.* And what if winning requires lying? What happens when lying becomes normative? Was it always normative?

"There are lies and there are lies. Some add colour, some injure. Can we tell the difference? There are ways of lying that thin personality, thin society.

"Winning justifies lying? And if to win is a lie too? Yes, there are enemies out to get us. I don't want to be ruled by them or killed by them. But it is possible to be destroyed by our own leaders, to be destroyed by winning. Winners and losers flatter themselves with the claim that righteousness justifies destruction.

"At what point does winning bloat? At what point does it thin the feel of life and turn us into splinter people? The way we win chips away at the fullness of being.

"We are extinguishing the fullness of ourselves. Becoming narrow funnels of hate or profit. Is what's happening too frightening to address on TV in a real way? Here, in the land of plenty, I see constriction in the face of winners, as if winning makes them smaller, makes their soul wince. We are being conditioned to ignore.

"A male patient dreamt of a heterosexual couple. The woman, especially, had a full, open body. Immediately after this, he dreamt of two men, gay men he thought, with a solid, full, open feeling too. The dream gifts him with a sense of being that makes life worthwhile, that makes being human worth it.

"It's unusual for him to have a dream without a negative turn. It's a reprieve. The guillotine didn't fall.

"Then a downturn, not the worst possible. A scar was smarting. Someone was disappointed with him. A professor who asked him to preside over a big meeting in a big hall. Something didn't work, he wasn't sure what. He felt apologetic, ashamed, more comfortable with small groups. He'd rather be off to the side, not a main event, not a big deal. He feared he failed his trust. Then found the professor's lost keys in the ground and felt, 'God did this. God showed them to me.' He pictured giving them to the professor. For the moment, triumph over omnivorous bad feelings, a bit of redemption.

"He smiled when he told me these dreams, then dropped into silent awe, or so it seemed to me. His lips quivered when he told me that the muscles in his back were twitching like bugs crawling inside him. He saw a man—himself, his professor—hanging from a gallows.

"And what do I, the doctor, want? I wish I could prevent death and cure terror. I feel small next to my patient who feels small next to his professor who hangs from a gallows. All so small next to the great forces of life. As you must feel small next to me, wishing there were more you could do. Only ourselves on a gallows falling into a dark well radiating well being."

*   *   *

Grace: "I fell through the hole in whole. Ha-ha, you think I'm joking, being smart. I know you secretly get annoyed when I'm smart-ass. You tolerate it, wait for it to pass. I do the same for you. It's annoying. But if we cut each other slack, sooner or later something happens. I wonder if something will happen today.

"I am thinking of the Wrong, the Wrong in Itself, a Kantian, Platonic Wrong. it is my essence. It is mirrored back to me in the news.

"A girl killed by her stepfather. A picture of her tied in a chair, eating dog food, beaten, starved, thin as a feather. The usual uproar, investigation, jailing. There is a story about her mother in jail weeping, saying she's a good mother. Each day the paper adds another story and then it will vanish.

"Did the mother and her husband try to kill the Wrong? It is a knot: people try to kill the Wrong but the Wrong kills people. To say I see myself as that girl would be an injustice to her death. But she is in me. I am a lucky her, alive in this room with you, with your Wrong, our wrongs together. We are lucky because we leave each other after forty-five minutes, we dose each other out. Time protects us, lets us tolerate being wrong together.

"Wrong meets wrong. We survive this meeting. In so much real life such a meeting blows up, crashes, even leads to death. Wrong against wrong, an excuse to kill. War takes over and sweeps people along. What led to this girl's murder, what swept them along? It takes less than forty-five minutes to kill someone, but with her it built up over months.

"A story said she was rambunctious and instead of giving in to her stepfather's shaming, like I did to my parents, she got worse, troublesome, obnoxious—and he killed her. She died rather than give in. I gave in and became crazy and am here with you today.

"Devil inflamed devil. A little girl's cheeky energy inflamed tyranny. We are attacked and attack back, whether or not attacks are rightly aimed. The energy of a little girl and a maimed adult. Not exactly a mini-mirror of aggression-to-aggression on the world stage, but not totally removed from it either. Personalities wronging each other, without resources to meet the wrong.

"Do we really survive each other? I said we do, but I spoke too fast. We survive partly. It's not survival here but change. Something happens for the worse. If we go far enough into the worse, we change. Wrong never goes away, but something happens when we grip it. I go into your wrong, you into mine, I find mine through yours, you through mine. To touch the worst. Most people most of the time try to get out of it when the job is to get into it. Freedom is working with the Wrong. I feel free when I don't have to make believe I'm right.

"My parents made believe they were right and I made believe with them. I have a paralysed brain. When I was little, I had so many scary dreams, murderers, spiders, witches, devils. One I had over and over: shit everywhere. Everyone was angry and I was ashamed. They wanted things to be clean. I was like the girl the stepfather killed, messing things, spoiling things. Now I see a grown-up world with shit everywhere, wars, deaths, spoiling the world we live in. It's not just me. The feeling it's just you is so deep, but it's *us*, *we're* doing it, our shitty selves, our shitty psyches. It's as if my childhood dreams are being dreamt and lived by everyone."

*   *   *

Grace: "I dreamt I was running in the night. A road in a college campus. There were students around, maybe a talk, an event. Suddenly a dog jumps on me and holds on to me and runs with me. We run together. It is very awkward. We could tip each other over. I am afraid he will bite me. But he is a friendly lap dog, and although he doesn't lick my face *too* much, I fear he will. I think of breaking away but the dream ends with us trying to run together with fears. The fears were mine. The dog was simply desire, excitement.

"There you have it, a rambunctious dog, like the rambunctious child I was speaking about the other day. Fear of being messed up, licked, hurt. My instinctive response was to break away, get free. I was being restrained, held on to. At the same time, the contact held my interest. It's not everyday you run down a street with a dog on its hind legs holding on to you. A kind of partner. As a kid in school we had partners for everything, standing in line, going to the auditorium, going to gym, running around the field together.

"Dog energy. I was a lap dog with my parents. Nice baby, nice doggy, good doggy, cute doggy. For me, dogs symbolize affection with a bite. What happened to my bite? I grew up biting myself. Now I can't get affection and biting right. The dog in my dreams is forcing itself on me. I have a choice to get away or deal with it. I'd better deal with it.

"Would I be a friendly dog, jumping on people and licking their face if I let myself? I hold back, modulate. Maybe babies are more like that, or parents kissing babies.

"I felt alone in the night. The college students were on the side. I was not one of them. Always somehow alone. Alone with a dog who comforts and scares me. I'm always the odd one out. A biting, affectionate person who doesn't belong anywhere, running through life rather than running into life. This time a bit of life runs into me. The dog has a real impact. I have to notice him. I can't just run by. If I break away, it's me breaking away.

"As I am telling you this I feel like I'm coming back to me. As if my identity was gone and I didn't realize it and it's coming back as we speak. As if the dog is warming me up and I am warming up talking about being an affectionate, biting person. You are my doggy, too. We are affectionate, biting people, you and me. We run together, isolated together away from the rest of the world in this room, different. Not many people want to hear a crazy person or hear what's crazy about a person. And when I'm speaking like this I don't feel so crazy. I feel there's life here. Outside there's make-believe."

*   *   *

Dr Z: "The environment is part of our body. When I go hiking and feel the beauty of the hills and lake, my body feels better. It blends with the setting. The world enters my pores. When I'm by a sick lake, my body mirrors the sickness and becomes a polluted body, a clogged body. A body responds to the health of things. Taste, touch, sight, sound can be healthier or sicker. Do you think there is such a thing as a healthy colour or sound? I *know* there is. The sight of how things grow makes a difference. We take in what's around.

"'A sight for sore eyes', we say. What we see makes us feel better or worse. You come upon a beautiful spot in the woods and dull-ness lifts. You see again. The smell of the soil changes the taste of your body. You get quiet enough to hear the birds. You hear the air. You think the air is breathing. How cramped you were without knowing it. You didn't know your body was hurting.

"In the city I clench my teeth, brace my back against the noise, the dirt, the speed. In the woods I listen for someone who hasn't spoken to say something I've been waiting to hear.

"I dreamt of chickens in a cramped space and thought about my cramped life. The next night I watched a TV report about chickens with their beaks cut off so they couldn't peck each other to death. They were stuffed together for egg laying in disgusting conditions. The scene switched to crowded prison conditions. Research showed that prison education programmes cut return rates and the government cut funding for such programmes. An official asked about the funding cut said there was a fear that people would become criminals in order to get a free college education. I suspect it was more a desire to treat criminals like chickens.

"Education doesn't seem to stop criminality on the top of the ladder. When Renquist died I thought guilt killed him. It's said that conscience can kill you, and maybe it can. To stop the vote count for the President of the United States—is that how you'd want most people to act?

"There is a secret need to be a human being and guilt for not being one. Some kind of selective disconnect is part of normalcy: not caring for the welfare of strangers or enemies as much as you care for your own. But it doesn't speak well for normalcy if the top judge of the land disconnects from caring for justice. Isn't justice about going against the "normal" tendency to be biased, the "normal" drive to be on top, to win no matter how? Isn't justice about justice? Precisely not to favour a viewpoint because of self-interest, to remain open to claims of competing views, to fairness? Don't you think an individual committed to law must feel shame at betraying it? To be the head of a court that feeds claims of power over democracy? Sometimes we die of self-disgust.

"Perhaps such a death is testimony to something good in us. As if we could not bear another poisonous moment. Another self-poisoning moment. Societal poisons leach into the body. There is emotional air and soil and what we do and think and feel impacts on social atmospherics. Together we create the social air we breathe. Our taste affects the taste of the earth and the taste of the earth affects the way we taste each other. We disconnect from our disconnect, but social atmospherics are real and take a toll.

"Is this nuts? A criminal supreme court is bad karma, sends shock waves through the universe. Part of the shock in motion is 9/11. It's a process very much in progress, with counter-ripples. Waves and counter-waves. Without a clue what's next.

"We once thought truth was a cure. Now it's part of the disease. The enduring pandemic is the wrong we do each other. Law itself is part of the virus, part of terror. Crime attracts crime and tells us something's wrong with how we approach power.

"I dreamt I was trying to get into a meeting but the door stayed locked. It was a breakfast meeting, people gathered together. Finally, I get in and see the people seated at tables talking and eating. It is a library-like setting. The meeting will soon begin. For a moment I felt I didn't miss out on anything this time and there was a nice feeling in the group.

"Then the dream turned into something like my patient's. An old professor of mine read a paper I wrote and praised only the Shakespeare quotes I made. I was proud he read my paper, but I can't compete with Shakespeare. Mind puts self up, puts self down, as if in competition with itself. Innate deficiency curls underneath attempts to outrun it. We are amazed at great things we do, sticking out our tongues at the pull-down. Shakespeare is a great thing life pulled off on one of its up cycles.

"As a human being, I feel a little reflected glory. But the wrongness doesn't stop. An eye peels skin off skin of layers of self, psychic skin. Very little is left. Something in this process wants nothing left, nothing at all. But that is a dream that cannot come true. There are dark spots, blank spots.

"I've got to tell you I am suddenly very happy, inexplicably happy. Why, I don't know. It spread in my skin, I think from my chest. I am in the wrong. I mean that literally—inside the wrong. Deep in the quiet of the Wrong. From the special spot I occupy I can only see one thing: layer after layer dropping away. Layers of Wrong, I must conclude, but don't really know. Layer after vanishing layer. And as the layers vanish, happiness grows. I think I'm going to end the session laughing. So many troubled areas waiting for attention and all I can do is laugh."

*   *   *

Grace: "I went to a lovely restaurant last night. The first course was so good. Then the waitress vanished. The service ended. We waited and waited. I was having a good time so didn't notice the main dish was taking too long. Should I make a fuss, express a grievance, or wait it out? I didn't want to create a disturbance and spoil a nice evening.

"Then I thought, asking what happened to the food wouldn't be creating a disturbance. It's just a question, a reminder. I got more and more annoyed, afraid to ask. I was on the verge of ruining a good evening by not saying anything or saying too much. Couldn't I just say, "How's the food coming?"

"Even if I pressed them and said something sarcastic like, "Forget about us?" or "What happened to the food?" or "Something wrong?" it wouldn't be the end of the world.

"Inside I felt it would be—the end of the world. How to preserve the overall good feeling yet express a grievance became a major problem.

"Not being able to solve the problem of whether to speak or not or how reminds me of a night I came out of one of my hospitalizations and stood by a street lamp on a corner, suddenly seized by grief over humanity, the whole human race. I was weeping and people looked fearful and concerned. I must have given off stay away vibes, because no one came close to help me.

"I saw humanity and the ages pass before my eyes. The grief of humankind from its beginning, all the pain of life, all time condensed in a moment of agony. I cried and cried yet felt very good, deep in contact with myself. I felt in contact with deep truth, deep life.

"When it subsided, I realized there was a vast distance between what it feels like inside and the outside world, a chasm that could grow and grow. I had an inkling that if I went all the way inside I'd be back in the hospital. It hit me that all the contact with yourself in the world won't necessarily enable you to make contact with the outside world. You could as easily go farther and farther away while people and things seem less and less real. I haven't gone that far. I feel life is real even when I feel it is not. I don't think I could reach a point where nothing is real, but you never know.

"I need to find a way to keep the inside contact I have, to further it, yet link up with life outside me. It may take my whole life to do it or do it well, if well is possible.

"I got fooled by the feeling of newness. I used to think feeling new meant being new. Now I know the trap of thinking you are a new person. You think you are transformed, but that is not you. You think: this is IT. But it fades and you are you. You are you with maybe a little more IT. "I cried and cried when I realized I'd have to lose my new beginning. Then I thought, well, you don't exactly lose it. It's that you're not so fooled by it. It can be there, part of the mix, but not a pretend substitute for the whole mix.

"Instead you say, "Well, here I am. Here I am." And where does that leave me? Now I'm *me*, looking at *you*. Not bad, huh?"

*   *   *

Dr. Z: "I had more lecture dreams. In one I gave a talk on fear and trauma at the New York Psychoanalytic institute. I was welcomed by important people, so felt better, fuller, and spoke on the om/shalom effect. We touch each other with our feelings and resonate with trauma and peace. Human touch calms, especially if there is a sense of connection and caring between people. We carry emotional fields with us and our fields interact.

"I went on and on and didn't mean to sound too goody-goody, so spoke some about our need to break away from each other, joys and pains of difference. I kept trying to communicate a balance and felt I couldn't quite get there. I became more strident, almost shouting about the goodness of chaos and irresponsibility, the importance of chance in feeling free.

"I woke up feeling so alone, almost to the point of tears, beyond tears. I remember all the years of blaming my wife for how alone I felt in our marriage. Now I know it was me, the most alone one in the universe. No amount of blame makes aloneness go away. I'm not the only one who is the most alone one in the universe. I've met many most alone ones and heard of many more. Deep inside I fall into a well, and inside the well I feel there is no end to unhappiness. Then I am in another well, one with bottomless happiness. From well to well.

"Do I give talks to feel less alone? You'd think that makes sense. But after a talk I feel more totally alone than ever. If I'm lucky, there's a momentary rise of satisfaction, then the void. If unlucky, just the void.

"The truth is, I like my aloneness. Alone the word has one in it. The alone one, towards the One. Sounds a little mystical. This may sound phoney to you, but my love for my wife is growing. I feel our being together so long is opening me in ways I didn't dare expect.

"In another dream, I'm giving a lecture from a bed in the back of the room. It is a bed that someone, a colleague, is dying in. I am lecturing in the bed he lies on to die, his death bed. He must have gone out, left it empty. I'll give it back when he returns.

"My talk does not go smoothly. I am awkward and shaky yet feel I am preparing for a Big Idea.

"Then it hits me, something like: I wish you to be exactly what I want you to be and act exactly as I want you to act. Any deviation from this is unbearable."

"When I woke up I felt I discovered a basic principle of life, then slowly remembered Freud, my dream caricaturing a little portion of his writings on His Majesty the Baby, wish-fulfilment and desire. Tyranny is in the genes, in the psyche.

"His Majesty the Baby plays itself out in governmental narcissism, the megalomania of Numero Uno, greatest nation, greatest show on earth. The whole world should conform to Number One's wishes. OK for circus illusion maybe, devastating in real life.

"Saw Cindy Sheehan ejected from the State of the Union address for wearing a T-shirt with the number of American soldiers killed in Iraq on it. You know what would've been great? The next day all the so-called Democratic senators should have worn T-shirts with searing numbers.

"We are screaming for justice below the leadership and cannot break through. Nothing new. Was it Diogenes who was said to walk around Athens with a light during daytime looking for an honest man?

"Justice is for sissies. Real men make their own rules. Power is the name of the game.

"Why is it we feel so good when a Fitzgerald brings charges against a Libby? When a DeLay steps down? A slight crack in the soundproof system, a hint that not all is commandeered or high-handed. Justice lives in the cracks of power. We recognize a hint of justice by the immense relief it brings. Corrupted yes, but not entirely dead, breathing somewhat. To feel fair play is alive, no small thing.

"To object to foul play in politics is not simply a sign of *naïveté*. It is an expectation of something better. It is an expectation that how we use power must evolve. This is a trauma I lecture on: to be betrayed by those who are supposed to protect you, by those supposed to help. An ethics of fairness *vs.* a narcissism of power. Count votes? That's for losers. Winners don't need to count votes. They fix machines, polls, registrations, courts. They know how to win—and rub it in.

"This is not a healthy wind, a radioactive mood. Killing, stealing and lying is not the way to unify ourselves. Take from the poor, give to the rich? Bomb the asses off the bad guys? Our neighbour is our enemy? Kill first, love later. Was Jesus' message winner take as much as possible, if not all? Is this what holy books come to, narcissism of winning?

"I don't believe it."

*   *   *

Grace: My meditator says, "Go back to a safe place." But there is no safe place. There was no safe place in my house, no safe place for feeling. My meditator says, "Find someone to comfort you." She means a comforting presence within, a residue from childhood. "Picture someone who comforted you. Feel the comfort."

"Are you kidding?! I break down in inconsolable fury and grief. Did she say, did I imagine it, "Don't go back to crying." She did say it. She was worried. Or disgusted or frustrated, impatient at my being stuck so long. All my life there is this hole in the ice and when I fall in—and I do fall in, often—there is danger of a chill that will never go away. Ice on the outside, chill on the inside. Thermo- what do you call it? Thermo--something bad.

"I hate my outside chill, stiff skin, tight face. I don't think many people *really* like the way I look. I don't think I make many people feel comfortable. I think some appreciate a certain nervous intensity. They sense I'm in contact with something, that I have something to offer, something mad perhaps. Something to offer a little like a poet might. Some thought or word from somewhere else.

"I see people watching me dig into myself, through myself, through the ice, deep under. To say I might drown misses the point. I am drowned. I'm a drowned person. I speak from under the ice, within the thermocline.

"Do you know what a thermocline is? That's the word—deep chill. A chill that once was feeling. Horror perhaps, sorrow, despair, giving up, never giving up, fighting in the freeze, through the freeze, with the freeze. Is this the angel Jacob wrestled with—or did he have a warm one? My angel is a thermocline. I wrestle with my thermocline.

"If I go back, like my meditator urges, it's to shutdown. I tell her there's no place to go back to that's worth going to. She says, "Then let yourself be comforted *as if* you had been." She imagines you can imagine comfort even if you've never had it. She takes comfort for granted.

"To hell with her. Let her be alarmed, irritated. Niceness is not nice enough. I smell vanity. She is hurt that she cannot be a comforting presence for me, that there is someone she cannot comfort. Failure of a human or spiritual power she thinks she has, wants to have; she has for many but *not* for me. With *me* she is still a spiritual wannabe. I torture her by being an exception. She can't endure the torture scent that comes from me. The torture that is me may not be something she can know. She may be too well meaning.

"I come to the end of her personality and she of mine and break down and sob.

"Too much!"

*   *   *

Grace: "I dreamt of a tiny baby. It is very tiny. I hold it. It is mine. It makes me more secure, related, comfortable, fuller, whole. I think all things are made of chaos and a baby comes of it. Tiny may be all I can handle. But now I do have that—for this dream moment. A moment I didn't have a moment before.

"A baby survives the thermocline.

"I think I'm saying that a birth is greater than death."

*   *   *

Dr Z: "A colleague told me a dream in which she had the most fantastic sex with a stranger. It went on and on. At the end of this amazing weekend, she had enough and wanted to get back to her daily life, but her partner wouldn't let her and tied her up. From wondrous sexual freedom to captivity.

"She kept her wits and when he wasn't looking found a way to escape. Here it is in a nutshell. Something wrong always happens, even when things are perfect, beyond perfect. From mind-blowing grace to capture, restriction. The Garden of Eden over and over. There's a reason we're still interpreting it. Life's not usually as clear as this dream. Things are more mixed, baffling. Even in the dream, my friend had enough garden and wanted to get back to ordinary life.

"The same morning that my friend told me her dream, I dreamt I was in church hearing a sermon about doubt and freedom. There was uncertainty in the air, something fuzzy, unresolved, like the feeling of dreams in which you never get to where you're going. It felt like the church air, stirred by the talk, was filled with oscillating thoughts that didn't have anywhere to land. Still, I left feeling more or less OK. My brain a bit tingly, quizzical, wondering, thinking, 'You see, that wasn't too dogmatic.' There was a stream outside. It reminded me a little of Florence or Venice.

"Then a glob of spit landed on the back of my neck and hair. My first thought was someone spat at me from the bell tower. When I looked up, I realized the tower was too high, but I couldn't shake the thought that the spit was aimed, intentional. Like Al Pacino's Shylock, spat at in *The Merchant of Venice*. In the movie, it was a direct spit in the face, establishing the place of a Jew. "How unfair, how real," I thought. I was mesmerized by the great tension in life between fair and unfair. In the dream, it was my back, showing at least some circumspection, some fear.

"There was fear of disease. How to clean it off? What kind of germs did it carry? In the dream I think I feared tuberculosis. I think now the disease is destruction, hate, shame.

"Did the one who spat at me imagine he was protecting himself from a Jewish disease, the Jew in the church, the Jewish scapegoat? He shamed me so I would know my place? He put his bad stuff into me so he would be clean, high, above?

"But it is my dream, me. The spitter, the spit, the spat on. Spit and spite—shame. Am I unworthy of being in church? Unworthy because of my secret: a part of my mind that no one sees is above the human race spitting at everything? Spitting like a baby at my adult self. Spitting at my pretension to be a human being.

"Above everything, below everything. When you're one, you forget the other. In church I was reflective, moved. I didn't think of getting spat on. I didn't think I was Jewish. When my colleague was in sexual heaven, she didn't think of captivity.

"Or did she? I have patients who are tied, stuck, and forget they will ever move again. When a taste of freedom comes, they are surprised when the chains return. Oscillations can be rapid, slow. When life stands still you fear the earth will fall apart. If it falls apart, you forget it will reform. I don't know how to convey this, but it is exciting relief to live in the place where something else happens. I'm going to be quiet now. I don't want to spoil the idea of falling apart."

*   *   *

Grace: "I'm concerned that medications have toxic side effects. Antipsychotics can cause heart attacks. Antidepressants can cause brain damage. Yet other studies say antidepressants are good for brain cell growth.

"Damage triggers attempts at recovery. Brain tissues try to recover after stroke or seizure. Maybe they try to recover after medication. But what if medication never stops? You can't tell the difference between healing and damage.

"When I was in the hospital, I feared my brain was disintegrating. Was that medication or disease? Disease, I think. Dread of disintegrating was part of my breakdown. *I* was disintegrating. Sometimes it concentrated in my head, my brain. It spread all over. It was me myself disintegrating. I told a doctor, 'If only you could tell me my brain isn't *really* disintegrating, I could get through this.'

"At one point they tried electric shock and I blacked out. When I came to, I disintegrated. I literally saw the world in pieces, an awkward collage, my I a mosaic of tiles that didn't fit. They stopped after two or three tries. Thank God, they recognized it made me worse.

"I don't mind going through what I need to go through as long as I know it is *me* and not my brain that is disintegrating. If it is *me*, I can go on.

"Maybe that's part of feeling I can survive bad things. It's OK if bad things happen to *me*. *I* can take it. But that's illusion. I'm not sure I can take it at all. I *don't* survive very well. I'm used to not needing very much. All I need is my tiny portion, my little bit of damaged life.

"Medication helped to reassemble me. Disintegration receded. Maybe I lost an opportunity. I'm not sure I like the way I came back together. If I could complete the disintegration, maybe I could come back a better way, I'm a splinter, sliver me. There's disintegration in the background, a grumbling threat. There must be better ways to come together. Can I redo it, like breaking a broken bone that didn't heal right? A broken I?

"I got off medication hoping I could do it better. Everyone tried to talk me out of it A friend said I'd be doomed without meds. I got off a little at a time and made a great discovery. Meds or no meds, I'm me in one form or another, I'm the one who's there.

"Did I damage myself forever? Will the damage provoke repair? Eternal damage, eternal repair? I was hoping with no meds I'd disintegrate all the way. But once I was reassembled, it wasn't so easy to fall apart. There is something that tightens. Is it me who tightens or some tightening thing in me? Neither of us goes away for long.

"Sometimes I feel I lost a chance that will never come again. Yet I am part of my life. If I'm there, something is left. I plan to hang in there, no matter what.

"I'm better without meds. I have friends who go under without them and can't work with going under. For them it's too much. Meds bring them back. Somehow, I developed a knack for going under. I've discovered a secret buoyancy in the horror, horror as home, a home away from home.

"Meds made me come back prematurely. I have a preemie psyche. It's stiff and sore. Walls shift, crumble shifts. Something precious is there. I choose a sense of something precious."

*   *   *

Dr Z: "I was moved to tears by Reverend Lowery's oration at Coretta Scott King's funeral. He said it like it is. A fully human presence. What better way to celebrate the Kings than saying they would not support the current government's war or economics. Taking from the poor to give to the rich—not what the Kings had in mind. A questionably elected president with his wife in the background—they looked out of place with their pretend superiority, toughness. Small, if not for the power they yield. Contracted next to Lowery's fullness. He made goodness sing.

"Bush Sr tried to distance Lowery's power by joking about his 'poetic' language. Deep feeling pressures the psyche towards poetry. What a difference between mere economic power and authentic personal power. The power that comes with fuller humanity and the power that comes by suppressing it. You hear it in the tones, feel it in the gestures. One rings a bell in the centre of your being, the other makes you tighten, wince. One makes you cry 'Yes', the other makes you scream 'No'.

"I nearly shredded the *Times* today. What were the headlines? How the Democrats were defeating themselves! Not what a horrible job the Republicans were doing, not crimes in high office! The headlines made Democrats look weak, Republicans strong. A sickening media display, diverting attention, occluding concern.

"The omitted headlines, the real headlines? Administration Investigated for Illegal Spying. Republicans Investigated for Corruption. Administration Starts War Under False Pretenses. King Funeral Deeply Moving—Speakers Critical of Government Policies. What does the *Times* do? Instead of focusing on Government misdeeds, it writes about Democrat weaknesses. The former is haemorrhaging our country, killing people. Where is the media outcry? Where are the guardians of truth or sense, the watchdogs? Where is everybody hiding? Inside dollars at the top?

"What is wrong with this country! Does the *Times* really think that Democrat strategies are the sins that plague us? And the *Times* is one of our best papers! What happened to the media! Lowery wasn't afraid to say it like it is. But the coverage diluted its impact. Something awful is happening to this country and those who scream about it get criticized.

"If Isaiah came here today he would be laughed at. Those in power would say, "You must mean someone else. We're the good ones." To make lying an issue is already a sign of weakness. To want justice is anachronistic. Power defines justice. But there are better moments, breakthroughs. Martin Luther King Jr was such a breakthrough, and who he is and what he signifies, who Coretta Scott King is, gives the lie to power and the media that muffles the real.

"Iraq, Katrina—not just incompetence. Incompetence is too benign a word for systematic mayhem. Incompetence doesn't do justice to destruction as a political art form. It's not going to be easy to remedy the gutting of the voting infrastructure. I don't know when a president can be legitimately elected again. Tax breaks for the richest, pressure on everyone else. Economic gutting. Glut the top, gut the rest. Sooner or later the top will look down and nothing will be there but a long, long fall.

"Are they proud of their skill? Their great ability to make a fully human voice sound funny? Sooner or later it's got to boomerang. Sooner or later people will hunger for a real heart voice and get sick of mockery. The voice of material power mocks the heart, apes it for profit, position, but does not provide real nourishment. Sooner or later the heart will realize it is starving to death."

*   *   *

Dr Z: "And my fully human voice? Do I distance it? Mock it? Fear it? A fuller voice within? Some live it. Does everyone hear it? I used to think so, now I'm not so sure.

"Equality is for sissies. Winning is all. Is that the voice we listen to? Some listen to it not out of greed, but helplessness. We don't think we can do any better, don't know how to try. One gives up on a sense of loss that goes back to infancy, moments when it didn't matter what one did. Distress did not go away. No one came. And if someone came, it didn't help. There are pains in the background of our beings that never stop, that we don't know what to do with.

"Leaders promise solutions to things they can't solve. Hopefully, they will help to make life a little better. Often they make things worse. It can't just be that bullies win, those who push through the death in infancy and refuse ever to be helpless again. Who push others into the hole and climb over them.

"There are moments when one is all alone with one's pain, moments when pain fades into nothingness and one follows it. Something of a stupor tries to displace pain all life long.

"King's is a better model than the bully's—not perfect, of course. But he did not cause mass harm. He did not kill thousands or millions. He did not poison the nation's mind. He pushed through the hole of helplessness, acknowledging it. A power from the depths held him up, a deeper self came into the world. I'm not very good at it but I feel it, recognize it, support it. It's wrong to condemn oneself for what one can't do, if one can do a little something.

"I'd like to mediate that power too, with my patients, my readers, my colleagues, to create spaces where people touch their lives, little somethings that make a difference to the feel of life. One moment I feel helpless, the next I find room to breathe and move. I'm seeing more and more clearly that there is not as much difference between infancy and adulthood or family and nation as one might suppose.

"So often the world comes to a halt and starts again. So often one holds one's breath between the stop and start. A waiting bullies cannot do."

*   *   *

Grace: "My body is a war zone. Intense combat goes on. Missiles streak across my organs, making my skin break out in rashes. Maggots in my blood wait for a chance to eat through veins. I'm filled with tumours. I've had three face lifts today and already I'm sagging. I'm going to have liposuction. Or is it another kind of suction I want, sucking my psyche and making it better, making it go away.

"All is luminous. Light, Light, Light. But it does not make the maggots go away.

"Today I woke determined to go through Everything. Nothing would stop me. The attack came and I dropped into it, whirled. Today is the day I will go all the way. I will not end the agony with no end. This time I will see what happens. I will go with it forever until something happens. And if nothing happens I will not stop. I must find out. I must see what *it* is made of, what *I'm* made of. This is IT.

"No matter how hard I tried, it began to ebb and I rose above it, watching, wondering how this happened. It was familiar, being above. Something I take for granted. I probably don't realize it is happening most of the time. But this time I felt the difference, the contrast, being in it and above it. It's me both ways, double me. Single me as double me, double me in single me. Is that where the idea of Trinity comes from, one as three, three as one? Me being aware of me being aware of me?

"I became very tired and felt I've been tired all my life, psychically anaemic, not enough soul oxygen, not enough O, or too much

O. Asleep with one part of me and awake with one part of me, active and fatigued at the same time.

"You dive in and there is no end. There is no air and you squint and start to die and panic. It's like looking into a crystal ball and seeing war. You'd think I'd be happy but I'm humiliated. I mainly feel humiliation. I am not up to being me. I am not up to the job I set for myself, a total birth, a going through, a sticking with. I fall asleep on myself and it's all over. There's no chance of it happening again today. Maybe tomorrow . . ."

* * *

Dr Z: "Humiliation, Impotence. People feed off it. I'm supposedly one of the lucky ones but that doesn't stop humiliated rage. The spectacle of the great is humiliating. My own spectacle is humiliating. I'm a humiliation to myself. The smugness of power, infuriating self-importance. A humiliated, humiliating world.

"No one knows the beginning of soul wounds. Why are people who show them laughed at? Why are people who try to help them mocked? How did liberal become a bad word in politics—are we afraid of helping others? Maybe deep down people know that solving social problems won't solve the gravest soul wound. Soul wounds are deeper. Social problems that flow from them divert our attention. We pretend to know the source of injury but the ineffable wound of life scares us. And, like little children or certain kinds of children, we make fun of what scares us.

"One of the scariest things we do is cause injury in order to point and say, this is it. I caused it. You caused it. We know where it comes from. Then we can roll up our sleeves and attack a problem. We are doing something about it.

"Are we surprised the wound persists? The wound wounds us and we find another cause to fix. Fixing can make life better. We are obligated to try. But the wound escapes our attempts to fix it. It is what we most fear will get us from behind, ghosts that haunt. Wounds follow us.

"We can't shake ourselves off like a dog does water. Someone pays the price of all our shaken drops. To make believe we are not slipping on a banana peel mind is part of the kind of banana peel mind we have.

"If it weren't pathetic, I'd have to laugh at Cheney shooting his hunting partner in the face. There's a tiny glimpse of how we work. The wound will out one or another way. Almost comic, if a country and real people weren't involved. Our psyche finds ways to rub our noses in ourselves. Or other peoples' noses. Killing birds that can't fly, making a joke of it, as if death can't stand laughter.

"We fall into the great wound of the world as kids running through the woods. We don't know where it came from or how to fix it. One thinks it shouldn't be there, it's a mistake. One thinks it will go away because it's so covered with beauty. I pick myself up, not yet realizing I'll forever be a dwarfed version of myself, permanently humiliated by a causeless wound. A wound that makes precise mistakes."

*   *   *

Grace: "Many people have said that music is proof of God's existence, a direct line to God, oil of the soul. God seems to attach to so many things, menacing, loving, music one moment, disaster the next. If music takes us to God, what does art do? If music is proof of God's existence, art is proof of ours. Art shows what *we* can do. Music is awe of God, art awe of ourselves.

"A void is at the core of my personality, perhaps *is* the core. Under all the activity, the flux, the business—void. I've covered it with hysteria, thinking, doing. I've been fighting it all my life. Void scared me. I'm getting less scared of it. It's a relief to give in to its fascination, its pleasures. I thought giving in meant I would have to accept defeat. To feel it there without thrashing, to accept something would always be missing, that part of me would be missing. I had no idea how tingly being void can be.

"It's not just emptiness. It's more like I'm not there and not being there is a relief, a joy. Anxiety is another core. There's an alphabet of the soul, a psychic alphabet, a core alphabet. Void is one core, anxiety another. It's not that anxiety fills the void. It can try but doesn't succeed. The void continues beneath it, beyond it. Anxiety is a void of its own, a world of its own, a background nearly always there, ready to overwhelm. The void sometimes swallows it, tries to dampen it, shut it down. There are times when the void and anxiety fight to be Number 1. They fight for the same space, at the same time each creates space of its own. They are antagonists but also go their own ways, not bothering with each other.

"I used to attribute each to my parents—their anxiety, their emptiness. Flooding me with anxiety, leaving me empty. I'd fight and give in, lost and angry. Scared of anxiety. I'd fight it off, shut it out, as if it shouldn't be there, like a bug trying to thrash its way out of molasses. To open to anxiety. Is that possible? To open instead of fighting, open as well as fight. It's bigger than parents, more than me. Void and anxiety—a, b, c.

"My mind is chilled, frozen. It was easier in school. You read what you had to and found what you needed. My mind got knocked out by my marriage. Sexual madness followed. Relationships broke me as a person. I kept thinking something good was happening and then the freeze came. Something more than rejection or failure. Something broke me apart. The good in the universe became a broken thing and I tried to hold my broken insides together. The world looked like broken insides. Wherever I moved, wherever I looked, I was living in a world of broken insides.

"I remember the moment when reading became different. I felt the author's presence, near me, inside me. His insides in my insides. The first time it happened I got scared and put the book down. But I knew something important happened, something healing. It was a great moment when I realized that books were filled with peoples' insides and that their insides fed mine. A kind of miracle, to need an invisible presence, to want someone who is not there, who may have died long ago, whose words touch me.

"I fear the faultlines of personality will open and invisible presence pour into them. My personality isn't cohesive enough to have faultlines.

"There is music in the writing. It's not simply in the words. It comes from what is full in another person. It comes from another's void. When I feel that, my void is at peace.

"I'm touching a secret place I'd go to get away from my parents. It was a safe place then, but not always safe. Panic would flood it like a broken dam rushing over an old, dry river bed. Cores meld. Now this secret place feels like my deepest truth.

"There are outer and inner shells. My personality is an outer shell.

"It hovers with this interest, that hope, no peace in it. Peace is in the void. The void is big true, hysterical me is little true. Oscillating trues give birth to lots of trues."

*   *   *

Dr Z: "When suicide bombers blow up, it virginizes their soul. The soul becomes pure, clean, justified. Rid of dust and dirt, rid of being soiled. Maybe that's what they mean by getting lots of virgins in the other world, a feeling that they become virginal.

"Does all murder do this? To make a business killing. If you lose your money or win someone else's you say, I'm cleaned out or he's cleaned out. You clean yourself by losing.

"All the associations of money with dirt, filthy lucre, dirty or clean dealings. Money = shit. Freud associated money with libido, anality, sexual power and perversion, riches of pleasure and degradation, filth. Filthy rich.

"A government cleaning out its own country, making political friends filthy rich. Filthy soul, clean soul lose their distinction.

"A government laying waste another country. Waste—a process of analization. To spoil, soil, ruin. Dead and maimed soldiers—faecal material. A cleansing or soiling? Civilian "casualties". A frightening word, a telling word: to be casual about death.

"Attachment kills. Those attached enough to a cause, to a country, to put themselves in death's way, to "serve". *Service*, a killing word. To go to war for peace, for glory, dignity, or that famous term of the day, self-interest. To serve self-interest, to trick oneself, to trick and be tricked.

"Patriotism used to thrill me. Saluting the flag, hand on heart, drum rolls, singing at ballgames. Bombs bursting in air. Weepy thrills. Now the word sickens me. It's not in air bombs' burst.

"Attached servants funnelled through someone else's self-interest.

"It's a game that starts in the crib, the fusion of self-interest and attachment. Self-interest works through attachment, inside attachment, as part of attachment. The infant's interest in surviving, blind, driving. The parent's need for the infant to survive, parent invested in the thriving baby. A parent pours its personality into the baby like milk.

In so far as a parent's personality includes poisons, the baby's emotional milk includes poisons. War is a grown-up poison feed, a poison feed writ large.

"We speak of a baby fighting for life. War in the crib, in the womb, in the family. It doesn't stop. Yet, we are also permeated by nourishing forces. If we are here it means we once were centres of nourishing forces in the womb. We know what it is to be nourished and have within us a capacity to create nourishing forces in the outer world. Emotional nourishment to complement physical. To treat each other as psychic wombs, a new mutuality in service of birthing, to be each other's wombs in free, mutual exchange. Leave out the mutual and maintain one-sidedness and the process self-destructs.

"The great womb of life needs to be shared. Resistance to sharing is enormous. To claim the world womb as a possession is a kind of intimacy, a creative intimacy, but to exclude others from this claim is deranged, a madness we suffer from. One-sided self-assertion turns intimacy into rape.

"The world as outer womb. We explode it over and over, radiating what we try to create, substituting destruction for birth. Our leaders treat the world as if they own it, as if it should exist for them alone. A plague of grandiosity, the megalomania of power. For them, mutuality is a disease or expertise in turning others to fodder in the business of power, reward, waste. Corporate lies feeding on life replace monsters of myth and dream.

"And psychotherapy? What can it do? Provide compensation for not being able to do anything? To contact oneself, to taste differently, to touch a few others who come one's way, to open wombs, other doors. One thing in its favour: psychotherapy does not support a war based on dreams of empire. It supports exploring such a wish. It supports exploring wounds and grandiosity that move us to destroy.

"Living in womb or out of womb—both depend on quality.

"Where does war come from? Vanity is not the only answer. But never exclude it."

* * *

Grace: "You're not a void person. I feel your spark. I know you're withdrawn. Your face gets drained of energy, thin, contracted. It's a concentrated contraction. It's not dispersed like mine. I contract to bind fragmentation. It's not something I want to do any longer. I want to let the fragmenting go. I'm a fragmenting person. You're a contracting person, a condensed one. I'm a diffuse one.

"I know you're into radiance. I bet when you were young the pleorama meant the most to you. You have your voids, your nothingness, but that's not your value, that's not where you live.

"Maybe I came to you to release my void. You can let me be it, have it. You won't steal my void from me. You don't want it. You have enough on your plate. You can let me have what's mine.

"There are void people and fullness people. That we're together proves that different souls work together, *must* work together. I release you into your fullness, and you release me into my void.

"You pretend to know about the void. It's not exactly that you're pretending. You have an inkling. But it's not your strong point. You know enough to feel along with me. I'm foreign territory. I don't come natural to you. The void is not your thing. You're not into what's missing. You're into what's there.

"You're worried that I found you out. I know your secret. I will broadcast it and all will know. You will be embarrassed, ashamed. YOU ARE NOT A VOID PERSON AND I AM!

"When I was young I wondered where nothingness came from and was afraid of it. But there was no-me a long time before me. Nothingness surrounds us, encompassing everywhere. Nothingness is the primary fact, the medium somethingness lives in. Something in a sea of nothing. Nothing nurses something and is the Great Mother of all.

"Are you happy with your radiant cup running over? Does my emptiness and your fullness make a happy wedding? Insides to insides touch and what will be born? I can tell you worked long and hard to make room for nothing. Fullness hides it. I can imagine you suffered from void deficiency, as I suffered from fullness deficiency.

"You're hidden in the fullness of horror. No one would suspect what you're like from your books. You name horrors of the soul but make room for me. You want me to let myself in.

"I sense you sensing me and sense myself more. To sense myself, to formulate a difference between us. It happens in a flash, then springs into being. The delicious gulf that separates. Something new, something old, the greatest secret of all. Separation is not painful, it's ecstatic. Except for me it's nothing, for you a lot."

*   *   *

Dr Z: "I think I always knew that nations were mad. I don't want to die for mad causes—I don't want anyone to. Madness is part of who we are. It is important to say no to oneself, to say no to one's group.

"The child says no to its parent. Satan says no to God. No propels, says no to now.

"I am a premature version of myself. It takes a lifetime to grow into oneself, to become a home one can say yes to. Yes—the all yes, eternal yes. Does it always happen prematurely? No eggs one on, makes sure you don't throw in the towel too soon or for the wrong reasons.

"No is more than no to pain. It asks for self-overturning. You say no to who you are now. You go through more to be a better version of yourself.

"Nation abuse, child abuse. The same impulse runs through it. Abuse—self or other, big or small. Trauma competes with trauma. We worry that a cesspool of haters build themselves up by flooding others. What's right becomes food for what's wrong. Nation as engorged tick feeding on itself.

"This can't be the only truth. There's so much creativeness. But there is a lesion, a haemorrhage in bloated tissue. Our inner organs are drowning. We are thrashing not to drop down, pretending to be OK, flashing distress signals to one another, hoping for a gesture of recognition.

"We are reaching a point where recognition is not enough. We have reached that point already."

*   *   *

Grace: "It has cost me a lot but I have to be by myself. I can't live with anyone. The cold despair, the dread in the night is soothed when someone holds you. When the morning comes, you are OK again. But you know the dread is not gone. You've bought some time.

"There's no organ you can point to and say that's where the dread is. To think you can is a myth of science. Maybe they'd like to control it, but they can't. The dread they try to make go away makes them try to make it go away. They push it around, add, subtract, but the dreadful spirit persists. It comes another time, another way.

"It comes in the mutilation of war they are afraid to show on TV, that they show in make-believe movies, fabulous depictions that mimic reality. Movies put the horror of war in your face only to make it go away. It's out there on the screen. Not in you or on the street. What is it about movies that disappears reality by showing it?

"My dreams are filled with unseen presences that horrify without showing themselves. There used to be cut up animals in the desert. A spreading sense of all the peoples of the world butchered. Cut up flesh, untargeted pain. I would weep without a sound and no one would know why. I would weep for all humanity, all life. They wanted me to stop. But I saw the mutilation, the flesh. The blood of delicate things.

"There is no reprieve but there is silence. When I first came here the sounds outside the window burnt my insides. Traffic rushed through me. Wild animals came through the window, horns of blood and fire, flame-throwers. Burning children inside me. Fire is like air that skin breathes, pulsing from skin to skin, nightmare fires lit from things inside us.

"Do all fires in the world start inside us? In, out—does it matter? We pretend this is out, this is in. It's the same cruelty, the same madness. We divide it to try to live with it. Sooner or later, it breaks distinctions, shows us a taunting oneness.

"Once upon a time, I was with a man I loved but he didn't like to spend much time with me. Maybe he wanted to, but couldn't. He'd bolt in the middle of a word and say, "I've got to go." I somehow understood. I felt with him. I felt he had to go.

"I know what that's like—to have to get out, to just get out. I'm suffocating, drowning, falling through a trap door that's always opening under me, skinless, vanishing through my no. You can say a million things. But the fact is: you've got to go.

"I loved him more for being himself, for being honest. I felt at one with his need not to be with me. I cut him slack, as if he were another me. His leaving when he needed to made me trust him more.

"I didn't stop seeing him when I found out he was seeing other women. I thought, well, he's being himself, he's being honest. But I never felt the same. My trust wasn't big enough. I muffled the injury but damage was done. I refused to let it spoil the relationship but it simmered and there was nothing I could do. Even so, I didn't stop loving him. It was an injured love.

"The break was sudden, thoughtless. I met a man who wanted to be with me, to live with me. I loved him but not as much as he loved me. The cycle of time turned, and now I was on the other side. I needed space but didn't want to throw love away again. I loved both men and both loved me, but love distributed itself differently.

"Would this have happened without a wound simmering? Would I do it again when a new wound comes? I was angry at injured love, but is there any other kind? Would I drive my new love away by my need to be alone?

"I never worked it out. But it's been a long time since I dreamt of butchered meat and dismembered bodies. The faceless dread is there without the mutilation."

*　　*　　*

Dr Z: "Have you had patients who dream of famous people, especially showbiz people? Most patients don't on a regular basis, but some do. I used to think it a false self, a mask, some kind of grandiosity, a wish for fame covering a deeper sense of privation. Now I've begun to think of it as a kind of language.

"Some filter their personality through famous people. It's a way of making a semi-transparent floor above deeper layers of self, a way to see, even to contact those layers.

"I tend to see famous people in dreams as frozen. Something in the personality died and came back as famous. Famous people look alive. In show business they get paid for simulating life, portraying aliveness. They might even seem bigger than life. Sometimes you meet the real person and they seem a shrunken version of what they looked like on the screen. Their bigness is a way of feeling on top of experience.

"Theatricality is not just a defence. It is an opening. You see what's there, feel what's there. You make contact through the mask, while staying on this side of the mask. In dreams, famous people cushion psychic reality, although sometimes they seal it. Even if horror breaks through, it is staged, theatricalized, hystericized, mediated through a wall of success, of fame, of people you read about in papers or see on stage.

"It gives you a chance to know something is there, several times removed. A glimpse that defines a project: what you see through actors now, you have to feel for yourself later. That time may never come, or it may come a little at a time, in doses. You may never gulp the whole of yourself. Theatrical glassiness may harden inside you.

"It's not just: I wish to be like that. It's also: I am like that. I am the actor inside me, the dream actor. Inside my dream there is a barrier, a dream barrier. Theatricalization of feelings is a dream barrier. What is most intimate is a ploy, a smooth screen I can't pass. I can't get to the other side where the feelings are. There may be no other side. There is the sheen of feelings, glossy feelings, portrayed feelings. A picture. A dream picture of another person shielding me by freezing my feelings within himself. A not-me picture in which my vital life is frozen for safekeeping until some future time when I can come alive.

"Theatricalization of emotions. Politics is a lethal form of theatre. We speak of the world as a stage, a war theatre, play down the realness, make a game of it, look the other way as bodies fall off the screen. Theatricalization of selves, bloody theatricalization. Business suit theatre, business suit war. We theatricalize terror, sentimentalize murder. As if sentiment can justify things we do. Theatricalization of ideology, of ethics. We worry about polar ice melting but the truth is an ice age is under way. Our dreams are freezing."

* * *

Grace: "What a beautiful day! I walked here through the park. Warm as spring. Traces of snow on the rocks. Some people were sitting by the Shakespeare theatre sipping coffee. It was almost like an Italian town. I felt tearful. Full.

"You open a curtain and there is beauty, sunlight, goodness on faces. A reprieve. Waves of goodness.

"Thank you, thank you. Sweet and gentle thank yous well up. A perfect word: wells. To feel well, to be well. To be an unending well, a beautiful well that goes on forever. There will always be water in this well.

"I *can't* have breakdowns any more. Does that mean I feel deprived of them? I think it rather means that I am relieved of them, that I am now breakdown-free.

"I have avalanches, mud slides. I break down inside myself. I look inside and see a gingerbread man eaten by a wolf, running from a wolf, eating a wolf, running from a world. Puff: gone! Where are they? Have they eaten each other? Did they turn into violent air?

"The world is having a breakdown. Air is menacing. There is no psychotherapy for the world. Phoney sanity is the madness people notice. But phoney sanity sanitizes madness only so far. Real madness goes unnoticed. Real madness goes unnoticed beneath the impotent solutions of phoney sanity.

"Running from the world. Disappearing. Puff, I am walking through the park, smiling. How does this happen?

"I used to get hospitalized every other year, sometimes twice a year. Breaking down was my life. A way of life, an expectation. And now it is gone. My breakdown life is gone. I'm a little afraid to say it but: I CAN'T BREAK DOWN AGAIN. It is no longer possible. Something has been bridged.

"Attack never stops. But a veil lifts and there is more than attack. Something bigger. I aim at myself through crosshairs no one sees. It's like flying into the World Trade Center over and over. When it stops you think, "Why did it stop?" You keep crashing. Bad thoughts crashing. Violence everlasting. In your mind, planes keep crashing. THEY'RE NOT SUPPOSED TO STOP.

"Like sex, like breathing. To think of stopping is a violent wish. All wishes are violent. Non-violence is a violent wish but is better than the alternatives.

"Thinking has a limit when it comes up against a beautiful day. Thinking tries, but fails, to accuse the day of lying. Even if it succeeds, to say a beautiful day is a lie does not mean that all beautiful days are lies.

"It comes to this, then? Whether goodness I feel is real or whether it is the skin of a mannikin that is real only when it is blown apart.

"I stopped breaking down when I saw that breakdowns were a way to get blown apart."

*   *   *

Dr Z: "Someone whispers inside, 'Nothing is wrong. Nothing is wrong.' Makes bad things go away. Nightmares arise, disappear. You had a bad dream, only a dream. Only your life. Inside the dream of life a mother soothes her baby, making pain go away. It's all right, it's all OK.

"How does one break through the gauze? Where does fuzz come from? The way the brain works? But the brain isn't just conservative. It is revelatory. It uses lots of gauze to wrap the blood of insight.

"Womb after womb. We con and can ourselves, then split the cans and get born again, labour after labour. So many ways I've not let myself get born. It's not a matter of "let". Better to say I've not been born, I'm partly born, somewhat born in some ways, less in others. I'm in the process of being born. The best births are yet to come.

"When I was young, I put my father down for not making more of himself. He was a painting and drawing addict. My mother ran a business and made money. I took that to mean she made something of herself. She was assertive. My father was a cripple in this world. He painted his life away.

"I used to think I didn't put myself over the top because I'm crippled like my father. Mother egged me on, father held me back. I blamed him for my not being more. No matter how well I did, I blamed him for my not doing better.

"There is something crippled that cannot be repaired. Success does not undo it. Success did not make my crippled self go away. All the effectiveness in the world cannot make inner defect vanish.

"I am lucky to have tools to play with, to have got somewhere worth getting to. I picture two boats. I took the one that was ready to go, that got to its destination first. Then I see a second one still in the harbour. I look more closely and see kids playing on it. That's the one my father is on. Now I think, that's not so bad, spending his life playing on a boat in the harbour. Maybe he had more fun than my mother in some ways. Maybe his life had its own richness.

"His paintings are good. They've developed over the years. They keep developing, a little like a film in a tray developing over years. He has *that* satisfaction. To see his work grow, work that he is part of, a process he believes in. *Now* I can appreciate it. All my life he was the *irresponsible* one—that's what my mother and her family called him. *Now* I feel, 'My God, power to you—you mined what God gave you.'

"My changed valuation of my father gives me another perspective on why I am where I am, why I didn't ring the highest bell. Not just because I'm weak or self-defeating. I'm not sociopathic enough. I couldn't put my feelings aside enough to do what the next levels required. That's my father's heritage: to pay attention to what you feel and not ignore your basic self. I could only twist myself out of shape so far, then met a core resistance.

"I've done *some* twisting. Enough to keep afloat and get somewhere. Not enough to take on enough shit to sink. We move along our own trajectories. Enough compromise to survive well enough, enough realness for survival to be meaningful.

"When I was a kid, I always wanted to be outside. I didn't want to be with my mother. She was angry. We were angry together. I'd hide outside and my father would find me. To leave and be found, this marked me deeply. Now I feel I'm finding my father rather than the other way around. To value my father's values is a reversal. It sneaked up on me. It's changing me.

"It feels good not to know whether I am in harbour or at sea."

*   *   *

Grace: "I awoke holding the devil with both hands, kissing him hotly. Why do I say *the* devil, why not *a* devil? Why do I say *him*, why not *her*? Or *it*? You slide through language chutes and puff—a world of hes, shes, its, thes, as.

"Given, language slants it this way, that way. Narratives take hold where an event was or is. Here is an eternal event: hot. Kissing hotly. When fierce arousal grips, everything else is secondary. Hot. What more to say?

"To hold the devil with both hands and kiss him hotly. Everyone knows what that means whether they've done it or not. You don't have to know what it means. It happens. It goes on.

"For me? It means the end of paranoia, the end of fear.

"I'm thinking of identity rings. Rings of one self within another. Last night I went to Zen meditation. The leader rang a bell. You sit and the bell ripples through you, waves through your tissues. Delicately. My spine tingles. Shivers of being.

"You see your self, your selves going through you. Some almost stop and speak to you. Ripples of self. Ripples of identities, not defoliating so much as quivering, becoming less solid.

"The urge to get an identity in the external world threatens to stop the process: this is who I am. Identify me, know me, here's my card. Without this proof you will liquefy, turn to air.

"Meditation gives me the hots. I sit, I get excited. I let it pass through me. I think I'll swoon, pass out. Then I feel tingly, alive. I can't wait for more. It's a me-hunger, self-hunger. But what is this self? It's as if this special thrill replaces the self, *is* the self.

"It is a hunger for what meditation gives me. Stop the narrative here, stop the self. Be in the world of open. And who would that be, wholly open?

"In the morning I'm grinding myself against a devil. The hot of hots. Hot itself. And now I'm speaking of opening, unknown opening. It's been a big day."

*   *   *

Dr Z: "I'm thinking of elephants, the saying we have our hands on the same elephant. Maybe it's more that we're all riding some elephant or other. Or maybe we *are* the elephant we're riding. Maybe it's not about *same*. It's more like, here I am, my elephant and I, and I see you on your elephant. If you're not trying to run me down with yours, I probably look and say, "Nice elephant."

"I'm a scientist. At least, I began hard-nosed. Research-rubery taught me there's more wiggle room than I imagined. The more you get into things, the more wiggly they become.

"We once imagined a machine universe, rigid mechanics. Now the machine is flexi, a plastic that changes shape and colour. A bouncy, rubbery universe.

"Now it seems natural to think of thought as a form of energy, that thinking creates explosions. Where do we get the idea that we shouldn't be so violent? But we *do* get the idea.

"I see my child's face and don't want to hurt her. Through her I feel more than ever the preciousness that comes into the universe, that *is* the universe. And I think things should be better. But there is no way I can stop my daughter from experiencing violence, her own, or mine, or others.

"I can't say yes to injuring others. Yet, I injure, caught unawares, forced by my nature. Injury doesn't stop even if awareness of it pains me.

"As a young doctor I'd eagerly scan new drug findings: maybe one was discovered that could alter human meanness, coldness.

"A lot can be done with mood alteration. But no drug will stop what we do to each other. We will not stop viciousness.

"There is viciousness built into the system. It's not even wilful. It's part of the way things work. Even if we found a viciousness gene and modified it, the system would find a way to run over feelings to run up profit.

"I went through stages where I did everything I could to make myself a better person, to excise the vicious self and stop being hurtful. To stamp myself out of myself, subjugate myself, rip out meanness, tear cruelty to pieces. I read mystics about self-nullification and marvelled at so much eclipsed wisdom. They knew the problem existed. They tried to destroy destruction. Great tales of wrestling self in the desert. Tales from the past press from the future. We are still at a loss. But we are better liars. We are better at forming societies, governments, publishing papers and news reports to point somewhere else.

"What I am doing this moment is feeling the acute pain of hurting people. People I love trigger this most. But it goes farther. I don't want to hurt anyone.

"I don't want to, but do and must. This is what triggers repentance, the wisdom and scourge of religions. This is what makes one say, "I'm sorry." Not the pretend of childhood, adults telling you to say it. But the hurt inside when someone is hurting. The hurt of the pain you add to.

"You think of the poor killing the poor, the rich killing everyone else. You look away from yourself, then back. Your life adds to the pain of life. And what can you do?

"I sometimes add to the joy of life, too. Now I mainly feel pain mounting as I focus on it. The more I feel it the worse it gets. I think

I'm going to swoon, blot out, lose consciousness. Oceans of pain. There's no end to it. The only choice is to keep going into it.

"I'll never get back. There is only pain consciousness. I think of drinking, masturbating, going to a movie, something to stop it, tone it down. Words form: all being is a throbbing wound. Pain keeps coming and something tells me don't turn away. For once in your life don't flinch. For once follow it where it goes. These are orders. Follow the pain even if it makes a hole in my psyche. A hole in my guts, my brain, my heart. It blasts a hole in *me*.

"A spiritual wormhole takes me far from where I started, another world of me. Pain turns into heaven. Will heaven contribute where pain failed? Can *anything* make me better? My hunch is heaven will fade, change, and be absorbed like all experience. Violent me is waiting. *I'm still here.*

"I'm still here with appreciation.

"We can't solve ourselves but things happen when we try. There's so much. When someone says, we're this, not that—I'm suspicious. If someone says, "You are this and that is how to work with it," I think, "Did you go through the wormhole? Do you know what is there?"

"Something wrong opens realities. I have to be careful saying this. People will misuse it. But it's true, pain perforates soul and propels you elsewhere. Wormholes are psychic facts."

*   *   *

Grace: "I dreamt of a plain girl. You liked her. You rubbed against her, she rubbed against you. At some point I thought, 'He'll only go so far with a plain girl. He'll draw away.'

"I feel beautiful sometimes, the kind of beauty you wouldn't draw away from. Men reach a repulsion barrier then split.

"I guess I'm sensing you can be with me only up to a point.

"I'm glad you want to be with me at all.

"It's more than my abjection that makes me say this. I really *am* glad.

"Plain me. Beautiful me. We each have our problems.

"I know you'd draw away no matter what I look like. Everyone needs time to themselves. I do, too. I don't want you stuck on me all the time.

"I felt humiliated when I was very plain. I feared men would shit on me, take me for granted. Sometimes they did. But being beautiful isn't as great as you'd think. People look up to you, want to take you down. It has glories but robs you of yourself.

"What am I talking about? What choice do I have? Do I have a say in the exchange rates?

"Plain me, everyday me. That's who's here now. And beautiful me? It's a feeling inside. Sometimes I look at you and feel it."

*   *   *

Grace: "Maybe I'm cutting us some slack for coming and going, in and out. Do men know how much of life is in and out? Filled and empty? I feel like a baby. You suck at a nipple and fill up, then feel empty again and ache for a nipple. Do men know what this is like?"

*   *   *

Grace: "Do men know what it is like to go in one place and come out another? A penis in my vagina going out my mouth or ass? Sliding around inside, not knowing which way is up or down? Getting lost inside, following the ringing bells. Hide and seek indeed. Seek and find!"

*   *   *

Grace: "I didn't think the pain would ever end. Going in and out of hospitals. Intensity that goes on forever, then ebbs. Devils everywhere. Crying for all suffering beings, all suffering devils. Crying that there is any evil at all.

"What did I know? I knew life shouldn't be this way. I knew all the religions in the world meant for life to be kinder.

"I knew I was in danger and might never come back. Life is too sharp. Claws, burrs. Bleeding devils. Devils are depicted with sharp things because you can't stand being hurt when you're sick.

"When you're sick you see how things are.

"You cry for how things are. You have time to. You don't have to do anything else any longer. You can't do anything else. People take care of you while you cry for everything."

*   *   *

Grace: "Religions felt how cruel things were and became crueller. And inside the cruelty there are tears. Inside murder someone is crying. Religions torture people. Religious people think that torture makes you free.

"They torture you with a God of love.

"Why so many threats?

"When you're sick you see how twisted people are inside. How they put on a face that tortures others, a clean face. Inside the rack is tightening."

*   *   *

Dr Z: "Love of wisdom is an excuse for unsolvable pain."

*   *   *

Dr Z: "T. S. Eliot triggered an uproar when he became Anglican. How could he betray nothingness. Yet we got *The Four Quartets* out of it. And at the end of his life he asked to see Groucho Marx—and Groucho flew from LA to see him. What else do you want of either man?"

*   *   *

Dr Z: "Are poets suicide bombers? Are comedians?"

*   *   *

Dr Z: "You have a number to call to report child abuse. Where do you call to report nation abuse?"

*   *   *

Dr Z: "The I sticks out like a sore thumb. Throbs like a sore. Everyone can see it. It's me sticking out of me. I look at others and see their Is. I takes different forms. It's solid, the same I. It's liquid, becoming bits of other Is. Our Is lapping around each other, licking each other like dogs lick asses."

*   *   *

Dr Z: "Now, that's a denigration, about dogs licking asses. Psyches licking each other. Let me make it better, like bees make honey. No need to choose."

*   *   *

Dr Z: "I guess I'm talking about a double death. Not just physical annihilation. Animal consciousness is more at one with its body. Our I is a symbolic magnifier. It sticks out of itself and magnifies itself. It magnifies states, blows up what it passes through.

"I as telescope and microscope, immense magnifier of what it goes through. This helps it notice itself, gives life importance. But it magnifies death out of all proportion and makes for deaths all day long. I's magnified death anxiety—much worse than a body's."

*   *   *

Dr Z: "I think of Laura, a girl I loved long ago. She married, has a family, a life. We haven't had any contact for forty years. Yet, I can't believe she has her real life outside my feeling, outside my fantasy. I believe and don't believe. How can she be living her life and not be living it with me?

"I am amazed we are not together. It's as if *we* are married, had a family, experienced getting older with each other.

"Yet I *am* married, living my life, deeply involved with work and family. My real life with my real wife. I would not end it for Laura. My life is good enough for me. It works well enough.

"Yet, here she is, Laura. She appears in a dream, reminding me she is not with me. She is someone else, outside my life, another life. Yet inside me, in my mind.

"That's part of what I mean by being liquid. A liquid I. *I* am married to Laura, living another life, a life that never was or can be, yet something of it goes on. It goes on in me and beyond me. As if Laura had a thought of me last night and came into my dream, letting me know that I am in her too, another life of hers, a life we cannot live but goes on anyway."

*   *   *

Grace: "Do you think I'm psychotic to think that leaders of our country made a stock killing by blowing up the avian flu scare? That they made a killing with high oil prices and war? Disaster is good for profits. Is this part of my psychosis or am I seeing clearly what goes on? Maybe it takes a certain madness to see what's going on.

"Sane people don't notice or can't believe it.

"I'm so used to thinking all the bad stuff is inside me. Or inside my family. I'm not used to thinking I'm sick because the world is sick.

"But it's not such a crazy idea.

"It's an old idea. The devil was called the father of lies, prince of this world. Calvin and Luther called man bad, sinful. Freud blamed the id. I'm not sure we've found a solution or that a solution exists. Shakespeare knew we were the problem but what do we do with it? It's not enough to be "rational" about it. "Rationality" doesn't work. We say what we want is rational and that what someone else wants isn't. It's reasonable to invade Iraq and, God help us, maybe bomb Iran, and it's weak, irresponsible pessimistic, unreasonable not to. This proves that rationality is delusional. Or a wily appeal to rationality is a mask for destructive power.

"Destruction is the key. My mind destroyed by madness. If it's chemical, it's chemical But I see destructiveness in my family's veins, a family held together by toxic feeling.

"When I was a kid I thought *we* were the only sick ones. Others were better. Now my eyes are more used to the dark. I see toxins in the good ones too. I can't make the same divide between the healthy and sick.

"The fact that I survived my family means there was some good in it. Perhaps I'm wrong. Perhaps I'm an annihilated person living an annihilated life. Now I see the lucky ones are messed up too. The fact that they function better means they can do more harm.

"I'm trying to reach a truth I don't want to see. That we adapt to badness. We seek something bad to mould ourselves around, bad things as nourishment. Like feeding on destruction. That's not all there is to us but it's a big part. We make believe it isn't so, maybe because we don't know what to do with it. Nothing we've thought of so far works, not well enough, not as well as we'd like.

"Perhaps what we like doesn't have too much to do with it.

"Yet as a baby we like good things, good taste, good feelings."

*   *   *

Grace: "Maybe we don't get over the idea that we should get a good feeling from someone else. And if the other doesn't give it, we'll take it. Is this the basic criminal act? To steal good feeling that winds up bad? You can't force others to feel good about you, but you sure can force them to feel bad."

*   *   *

Grace: "Is there basic goodness in hell?"

*   *   *

Dr Z: "To always feel behind. Chasing, never catching up. I've dreamt of being in a little car trying to catch up to all the big cars ahead of me. Like the last duck in line. Going up a conveyor belt that goes backwards, against you. There's that sense, a pull back and down.

"I've heard some say that pull is gravity. You're always going against a downward pull. It gets elaborated in ideas, like Freud's death drive, or moods, a depressive undertow. You're pitting yourself against it, struggling to stand up, to rise. You offer resistance to a pull within you in order to live. You resist life in order to make a go of life.

"A word like gravity says too much, a scary word, a grave word. A grave pull.

"When did I begin to feel I was partly entombed, engraved? Morbid fascination is very real. Sickly succulence. It starts with death when are very little and the way we twist ourselves out of shape to stay alive. It starts with pain. We begin to die very early and know it, although it takes time to know we know it. I knew something was wrong very early but it took longer to discover I was set in a grave.

"Transcendence is part of life, more life, life's resistance to itself. Turning life on, turning life off.

"A patient came in putting himself down for his need for chaos. He dreamt of sculptured animals holding a building up, building stones. The animals came alive and as life filled them the building began to fall apart. He was scared that he did something wrong, that something awful was happening. Life causes things to fall apart. His life causes crashes.

"A child keeps trying to catch up, causing crashes. Life is too much and turns to stone.

"It's not just mythology, turning to stone.

"My patient is growing. The stones are alive. The animals are alive. Alive in a big mess."

*   *   *

Dr Z: "Fast things, racing by. Windy. Little things speeding up. I awoke with this feeling again. I am too slow for—I was going to say the world. But it is Life that is too slow or fast. And just right?

"What can "right" mean? Certainly not right in an argument, not one truth bludgeoning the lie of another truth! Right means something good here. A way life feels. Now things feel just right. Now I really appreciate the way things feel, the way things *are*. Here right is a matter of taste, a kind of taste, a way life tastes, a good taste. Here right is not a weapon, not I'm right, you're wrong.

"To race after . . . to try to . . . to . . .

"It's exhausting.

"No, not at first. It is exciting, thrilling. I suspect thrill is in the background of everything and sometimes it tips us towards it and says, you see, I'm here, still here, always here, and now you've found me.

"Here's what I think: life turns to stone as we get more frightened by it and don't know what to do with our fear. We get more and more paranoid until our fear and life point at us from the outside, like a gun pointing at us, ready to shoot us with all the life that turned to stone. All our inside life threatens to shoot us from the outside. Rage rises with paralysis and we remain forever angry at life and paralysed by it. We become dead stones of a building but retain some semblance to life. We look like animals a craftsman made with love.

"We grow around a dead spot, a dead spot made with love. A love stuffed with hate in the middle of the stone.

"Will someone pull the trigger? The gun that is always aiming at us, made with love and the deadness life made by hurting too much."

*   *   *

Grace: "All night I felt spirit presences. I dreamt of spirits coming in and out of my reality. One told me, "The attic door is open, if you want proof." I went up to the attic and the door was open. It could be a broken hinge, wind. It could be . . .

"My reality. I hate my mind for saying this—is it MY reality? Do I own it? Did I make it? Is it MY mind? My oh my, what can the matter be?

"I am getting into mind to get away from spirit.

"The point is, something is broken.

"The fountain of life is broken.

"The attic door is one door of my mind.

"And down in the valley, in the body . . .

"Spirits are having sex with me and I am having orgasm after orgasm. Something turns on and I can't turn it off. All this is happening with our clothes on. No, spirits don't have clothes. They can't be seen. Yet our clothes are on. It is our insides that are coming.

"So there is a fountain, broken or not."

*   *   *

Grace: "I love it when an image seems so plain, so everyday, but says something more, like unhinged. To be unhinged, unglued. 'Normal' people use these terms to express ups and downs of feeling. But I bet sometimes they get an inkling they are saying something more. Words speak of a great more all the time—hints of a great lack of mooring, fall, crumbling.

"A fountain in the crumbling.

"Where are the spirits coming from? Inside the fountain?

"[My] mind says fountain but who knows what it means. Foundation? Founding? Foundling? An orphan mind?

"Pain teaches love. Joy teaches love. Which is the better teacher? This is what I hate about mind, setting up choices. You can't say anything without tripping. Without freezing.

"Do you think the water ever really stops?"

*   *   *

Grace: "Someone is looking at me with an empty look that says, 'Do you think the water ever starts?' There are bad spirits all the time saying things like that. Maybe not bad, just speaking for what is real for them. Empty spirits without flowing water. They are colourless, made of no wind or breeze. Not even dry ice, no temperature at all. Not even blank."

*   *   *

Grace: "You can't really fit it all together."

*   *   *

Grace: "Images pouring out of an image womb. You feel it will go on forever. You have to invent fertility goddesses, always pregnant, always birthing, teeming. The too much, never enough of things. The goddess just does this. You can't see something grow from moment to moment. You can't see a moment. You wait. You keep waiting. The momentum and momentous grow very quiet. Tears begin to make an appearance, waiting for a pause."

*   *   *

Dr Z: "Do dreams die? Are there dead dreams? I know there are dreams that portray death, express death. I don't mean old dreams we shed like skin. I mean dreams that express a death in us.

"Not physically dying, although that may be part of it. Emotionally dying, pockets of inner death. I doubt we are ever wholly alive or dead. Painters have an easier time because they can portray deadness and aliveness in a single view. To speak is to lose one or the other but inside there is both.

"What I'm asking is if dreams that express inner death must be dead to do it. Must they be a taste of death to make it real? Isn't that what they are trying to do? Make our death real for us?

"It's the oddest thing, when we have a bad dream we tell ourselves it's only a dream. We tell children it's not real, it will go away. We mean *we* will go away. We *all* will go away. Our little children and us will go the way of our parents and their parents. Like shooting stars, or, if we're lucky, fireworks. If we're very lucky, we'll light the night sky for a while. We'll light each other's skies.

"So we're establishing there is nothing more real than a dream. The disasters dreams portray are what we feel inside. What we undergo in life.

"We are afraid of calling life a disaster, as if that makes it bad. That life is disaster simply states the fact of tumult, of crises. Now we know life *is* crises. We can't normalize crises or make them go away. We talk about the crisis of a fever. What Freud is telling us: we *are* that fever and outcomes of that crisis.

"The truth is it is like trying to negotiate with a fire that gets bigger the more you try to put it out.

"Let us simply say it: our dreams are truth. We are phobic about truth.

"I think one reason we are phobic about truth—only one reason—is we think we have to act on our truths. We learn we are living a lie and feel called to right things with violent acts. The truth I am learning all my life is that it is easier to act on truth than let truth act on you. That is what is at stake here—do nothing with the dream, let *it* act on *you*.

"I began to get an inkling of this many years ago from a patient's psychotic break. He felt impelled to act on his sense of truth and fight the evil he saw around him. At the same time, he clearly saw that if he followed this call, he would die. To fight evil everywhere, as he saw it, was an act of suicide. He would end up under a subway wheel or with a policeman's bullet in his head. To fight evil meant killing evil ones, and evil was all around him. It meant, really, killing the human race, perhaps finally, life itself—where else did evil come from? He would have to kill all life in order to be all good. The logic of the necessity of his own death did not escape him.

"His solution was 'wussy' but he tolerated it out of fear for his skin: psychotherapy. He was willing to lose his soul to save his life. Or so it felt to him for a long, long time.

"To me it was revelation. Not doing something horribly violent to oneself and others felt like loss of soul. To sit and feel the many strands of life—this felt like weakness, soul loss: to lose one's soul to find oneself.

"How does one get out of this predicament? By getting further into it. By not stopping where the stop signs are. By plunging through the steel, by liquefying."

*   *   *

Dr Z: "Wussy is OK. We'd be a lot better off if we let in our weakness, be with it. Isn't that a biblical point—integrate the weak, the excluded, the needy? A child shall lead them? Stop pretending we're so strong or know what we're doing. The bible's a mixture of murder and forgiveness. Why forgive? I suspect the deeper order is if we can get to the place where forgiveness lives, we won't have to murder."

*   *   *

Dr Z: "Always *if*—the rub."

*   *   *

Dr Z: "I'm thinking of my patient's stone animals coming alive. When the animals are alive, there's no need for artificial structure. You don't have to hold yourself together like a stone building. You don't need an external carapace inside you like a ligature. Aliveness takes its own forms. There is spontaneous forming in aliveness. Aliveness is a forming activity and pain and joy are part of the way it exercises its powers.

"Where does blame come from? It's not simply from your parents. It's part of what life does, the power of aliveness taking many forms.

"Why blame yourself for aliveness? Because it hurts. Because it hurts others."

*   *   *

Dr Z: "To be blameless is not enough either. We lead and mislead, chase after power not simply because it is pleasurable. We are afraid to wait. We are afraid the dead gun of our life will shoot us with everything we couldn't live. There is a desperation in living.

"Self-attack never stops. You change shapes with impacts, inner or outer. You never are sure what is really impacting or where it's coming from."

*   *   *

Grace: "Womb thoughts. Dream thoughts. Dreams as part of womb activity. Dream wombs. Everything starts off alive. Every- thing *is* alive. Black hole is a baby going under. Baby takes a hit, goes down. Disappearing takes time. Way down below all the water. When the baby reappears the hole is there. It doesn't stop most of us from living. We live around our holes and sometimes fall in.

"Dreams are like a respirator in an intensive care ward inside us. They help keep life alive. An umbilicus to the World Soul.

"I give birth to a dream. Do I? Dare I say I made my dream? Maybe it's the other way, I'ing part of dreaming, I as something dreaming births. We dip into dreams to taste our lives in the raw, as if we have a sense that in dreams we are naked, that dreams touch the truth about our basic selves.

"Dreams help keep psychic life alive but, like the baby, take hits, go under, get damaged. There are mutilated dreams and dreams of mutilation, glimpses of our damaged selves. But they keep coming, damage and all, monsters from the deep or moments of grace.

"It is raining and I look closely and every raindrop is a damaged baby. And inside the baby is a damaged dream. Inside the dream a damaged baby.

"Damage doesn't stop us. Dreams are psychic bodies, partly crippled. They say, throw away your crutches and fly, and there I am above the rooftops, whole, high. Soon enough the ground will swallow me and I'll be inside it, suffocating, below all surfaces. Gripped by trauma, limitation, vulnerable. You can't really stop where dreams come from. You can't escape seeing how gnarled you are. You don't outgrow being a damaged baby. You just grow.

"And my womb, my birthing? Psychic womb, spiritual womb birthing? These kinds of wombs never stop. They can't stop. You hit them enough, warp them, and they make monsters—human monsters. I see them all around me. They lead our country, create hells. Hells everywhere because dreaming is everywhere. Dreaming our wounds, our wounded dream wombs. Iraq is a wounded dream womb. My country—a dream eating monster. Big Business using dreams for food, gnawing at the insides of dream life, stylizing dreams for profit, mass consumption dreams, marketing nightmares. Living dreams with all their damage replaced by dream machines made by financial force, by money Is. Dreams denuded of dream life.

"And my womb, the Void? The limitless ever forming Void? The Great Void nothing can fill? Pregnant emptiness? Massive womb pollution, void pollution. Toxic Void part of Creative Void or

Creative Void part of Toxic Void. Which is primary? Is there such a thing as primary? And part, what can part mean? We know body parts in war. Organs for sale.

"Dreams part inner seas and are part of inner sea-making. Polluted, creative waters; polluted, creative dreaming. Soon dream fish will have no oxygen, the red waters slowly end life.

"My blood-stained womb. Suffocating. Wombs breathe too. But it is harder to breathe when it is being mutilated.

"Freud speaks of a dream navel. A navel with tangled root systems vanishing from view. The great umbilicus. Where does it lead? The roots are lights in mind, ideas not yet born. Feelings waiting for a chance at living. Can you bring thought babies into a world that deforms them? That eats them up and grinds them into the great war machine? Dream machine as war machine?

*   *   *

Grace: "A man on the street stops and says, 'Dreams are not yet for sale. Sister, can you spare a dream?' Has time passed him by, I wonder? Who is this dream beggar? What will he settle for?"

*   *   *

Grace: "Everything one feels changes the void.
    "Everything a baby feels changes the void."

*   *   *

Grace: "God separates good from evil then asks us to make it right.
    "WHO WILL MAKE IT RIGHT?!"

*   *   *

Grace: "Join hands brothers and sisters—touch hearts.
    "We rule each other by intimidation. Who can correct *that*?"

*   *   *

Grace: "Here is what I see. A man in pre-ancient times. In movies, a caveman. In reality, who knows where. He hits a woman. There are no words. Something happened. Maybe neither is sure of what or why.

"The blow is reality. Whatever evoked it is reality.

"Even if a fantasy is involved, something imaginary, like a slight or wrong look, it is real. Imaginary slights are real. Wrong looks are real.

"What led to a blow that caused pain to the woman—will we ever know? More likely it was something she did that he didn't like or something she wouldn't do that he wanted or maybe it didn't have to do with her at all.

"What kind of pain in the man led to the blow? And all this pain, real pain, where did it come from? Is this how the psyche is born? I won't settle for that."

*   *   *

Grace: "God says you will give birth in pain. I take it, psychic birth. And joy is painful too? Yes, joy is painful. But joy is joyful. Yes, joy is joyful."

CHAPTER EIGHT

Emily and M.E.

Everything less than murder requires oscillating uncertainties.
Let caverns open. The nameslide has begun.

Emily: A dead baby in a box, a lion roaring in a cage. My dreams today. Look at the symmetry. The sin-atry. It could be roaring in a rage but it was cage. One eye sees a dead baby, the other sees a roaring lion. Put them together, binocular vision, you get death, life, boxed, caged. Dead me, alive me. Imprisoned me.

Let me translate from object to subject: *I* am a dead baby in a box, a lion roaring in a cage. Do dreams put in third or second what is first person?

When I say I it is a puny *I* compared with a roaring lion or dead baby. I need an I that reaches all the way down to where I begins. It must reach deeper than I. For when I die it is not only I that dies. Death goes deeper.

Deeper than dead me, roaring me, imprisoned me. The cage, the box, the deadness, the life—O so much deeper.

On the way here I saw words carved in stone above a temple door, words that moved me to tears: "Do justice, love mercy, walk humbly with thy God". I must have passed those words a thousand times. Why did I *see* them today? I'm crying thinking about them. They say *everything* so simply, the truth of it all.

When I weep over this truth I feel the baby come alive, the bars melt. Everyone is afraid of a live baby, a lion roaring with life. Yet we love a lion's roar. It makes us feel the pulse of life. Isn't that what frightens us?

* * *

M.E: Dream of going down—stairs, balcony, banister, maybe like a theatre, with young guys my son's age, his friends, nice feeling with them. I had to go down a few times. I kept forgetting things. At the bottom by the shore, a beach, picnic grounds.

The dark of the theatre is light with life.

I ran up from the beach to the cabin we rented, leaving my young son playing in the sand. I broke my toe running with bare feet on stone. I ran blindly, rushing to get back in a flash before anything bad happened. Before he missed me. I was rushing, anxious, happy, alive with life. You break things when you're filled with life.

* * *

Emily: I know your tricks. You're making me work to get me involved, to get me invested in my life. Attaching me to life through talking, *jouissance* of words. You know I'm into origins, doubling back to where the I comes from. To go back again to one's starting point. I can do this all life long and never get into living.

I'm my own twin. I'm double, triple, multiples of myself. A fundamental alienation, a fundamental difference from oneself. One keeps trying to close the gap, stop the difference. It's scary separating from oneself. It's not just out of body, out of mind. It's out of I. I out of I and more than I, other than I. It's too scary when you let I go, like a balloon flying god knows where. Will you ever come back is a first question, but you learn you don't have to come back. You keep going. It doesn't stop.

You don't have to catch up to yourself because you can't. You can't catch *it*. I used to think the I was a net to sift life. It's not a matter of catching. Life can't catch itself. Life isn't interested in catching Is. I is a spontaneous creation. I just happens, a ripple of life. It's not a matter of knowing. It's letting creating happen. Knowing is part of creating, an amazing ripple.

Amazing is the key, the word I'm looking for. Amazement. With utter amazement, dumbstruck, awestruck. Can you believe this is happening? It's not a matter of belief. It's not a matter of belief at all.

*   *   *

M.E.:   Murder as a way of organizing chaos, trauma. Obliterate disturbance, blot it out. God's great reflex, drown them, plague them, let them vanish in a hole. I'm sorry I ever created them.

Then someone has to plead, reason, threaten, show God He's wrong. He hasn't thought it out all the way, He will shame Himself. A Big Baby soiling.

When a head of government says I'm doing God's work, the distance between I and God begins to vanish. The great reactivity of God is funnelled through political calculation. It is a frightening display, a perverse shock and awe when God combines with corporate Is.

Floods of products, war as product.

The downslide in my dream is a downslide towards death. Then I think of going up and hurt myself. Oscillation, necessary, hard.

Ms. Militarized, medicalized life. Ms hurt me. M is my name. My name is being robbed from me.

Murder as solution to disturbance. Moloch. Michael, the angel.

Everything blends, oscillates. The names Adam gave are sinking, giving way.

*   *   *

Emily: To gaze at the mother's face, a compass point. The? A? *My* mother? It is less my mother now than a mother inside, a mysterious mother of my own creation. *Its* creation, my being's creation. A mother my psyche made of many snatches of mothering, like nests birds make with odds and ends. Seeing mothers in the park, in a movie. Or not mothers at all, snatches of glances that make you feel good inside. You walk down a street and someone catches your eye by accident and there is a light quiver of happiness.

*   *   *

M.E.:   The word democracy on a downslide. It means death to many, life to many. You cringe, the way leaders use the word. You picture it filled with bugs, lies, lunacy. You hear the word and duck. Something dangerous is coming. The balance between the word as death or life is collapsing. Can the word recover? If not, another must take the place of what it once meant to convey.

*   *   *

Emily: I saw a bad movie about the Inquisition. What's good about bad movies is how true they are. What's even more chilling is how true the movie is *now*. Inquisition as eternal state. In myself, in you. Torture as a tool. It may be outlawed but it's everywhere. The way people speak to each other, try to beat each other down. Dialogical torture. You can't get away from it. Inquisitor, Accuser, Beater. A way things work.

Authorities try to injure those who stand up to them. Bad parents of the world. Do what I say or else. God help you if . . .

Always a link with God. What I want, God wants. I = God. Does everyone know?

It used to be do what I want or lose your life. Sometimes still is. Words hurt more than stones. Definition is violent. The Inquisition failed to kill enough Jews but succeeded in defining Jews for most people, an effective accelerant.

Today liberal is a bad word. It's put down by left and right. When I grew up it was a good word. We're living through an inquisition against weakness. To be an inquisitor means you're strong. You put down others, wipe them out. No one likes weakness.

How long does it take to see yourself through the eyes of persecutors? In childhood, not long at all. Inquisitors don't share truth.

*   *   *

M.E.:   A patient, Kent, struggles to keep down his negative core when he playfully laughs with his wife. They created a kind of game, she wanting him to feed her a piece of pineapple, he making her say please ("beg"). You'd think they were having a nice time, if you saw them from the outside. And in fact they were, up to a point. The point is war can't take much pleasure. Every little bit is a struggle. This seemingly innocent moment was a victory.

I say it was worth the struggle. He says yes. I say your saying that justifies my life. He sustained another second, touched by my being touched.

I *really* felt my life justified by this moment. You would have to live through years of murdering pleasure and joy to appreciate this. You would have to know how rare, how improbable, if not impossible, it is for him to not kill off hints of goodness, let alone a whole sequence. Laughter always is a sequence.

I understand impermanence and the good seed may vanish the next instant as if it never were. A bird eats it and it is gone. But it is also possible that a seed takes root and grows, although invisibly for a time.

This is better than the law of the father. It is better than crime and punishment or simply punishment where punishment *is* the crime.

To share a touch of grace, an opening in the chain of punishment, justification worth sharing. I forgot that I laughed softly a few seconds before sharing. Now that I think on it, the little laugh, a quiet laugh, was part of thinking on the exceptional feeling I had. I was taken by surprise by being suddenly clear as the feeling of my life justified by a singular event grew. A patient laughing with his wife. A patient who could not laugh. *I* have not heard him laugh till this day. He is *so* concerned with truth. But what kind of truth can it be without laughter? And now he has lucked out, touched by a reversal, a new hint of learning, playful laughter itself a truth.

Kent tells me he suffered an eternity of dread when I laughed. "Then you spoke and said the struggle was worthwhile. I am so sure laughter is ridiculing. The laughter of the torturer burning holes inside the soul. I would have gone crazy, completely insane if you didn't join me, support me. I can't tell you how amazing it is to feel your laugh interpret mine."

*   *   *

Emily: I feel the guilt and shame my leaders should. All my life, guilt and shame burrowed into me, no end. A guilt and shame I see no signs of in those who start wars where people die. Is that the function of people like me? To feel the omitted guilt, to keep a balance?

I feel sick. I'm ill and fatigue easily. Suffering doesn't help. Running away from suffering doesn't help either. Both wear me out.

I remember your saying "You better believe it" when I told you something important to me. You had me repeat it several times for fear I would not hear myself. You knew I might not let it in. I might not let myself in. I'd skate over what came out of me and it would be lost. Speaking truth, even surprising truth, is a way of getting rid of myself.

I wept when you said "You better believe it" and I asked you to say it again and again and you did. And you asked me to say my words again and again and I did.

It was a gentle moment, a strange use of the word belief, a gentle tap inside, to believe in my experience.

*   *   *

M.E.:   A patient tells me about a "weird spot" from which he sees others and others see him. It not only dislocates but rubberizes, so that you see the other's insides inside out and your insides are visible too in deformation waves. All pleasure is sucked up into these waves, stillborn and sour. Hatred takes its place and my patient swears that there is no pleasure in it, contrary to the belief that there must be pleasure in almost everything, especially hatred.

He tells me a hopeful dream about being lost and injured, bitten by bugs. He feels this is hopeful, because for moments he sees the bugs that bite him. Normally, this would frighten but he found it consoling. There really are bugs that bite inside us.

My fear is they will hollow me out before I am ready. But when is one ready? They will hollow me out like an infested tree and I will look beautiful days before a great wind hurls me to the ground. People will see the dust and say, "He looked beautiful in the storm."

*   *   *

Emily: When I was a little girl, my mother died. The woman who took care of me told me, "Don't get too attached to her, she's dying. Soon you won't have her." She told my mother the same thing, "Soon Emily won't have you. Let her go."

Something inside told me this was awful and I curled up inside. Curdled feelings. What a horrible thing to do to a little girl, to a dying mother. And inside I dropped and dropped and dropped and became a blur. I've not spoken since. I've not made a sound. Even though I can't stop talking.

"Don't get attached to your own life, you're not going to be here forever," you said. I cried and cried and almost heard my crying.

A cry that split me open. Torn open by something past grief, torn open by rage.

Bits of rage well up when I see Bush's impish face, a face others feel is honest. It makes me feel violated. Maybe it's just a sense of violation ringing bells. To kill people, to kill feelings for a dying mother. To substitute smugness for experience. To displace caring. To say one thing and mean another, to put one over on the souls of children, to betray the core of life. For a moment, as a child, to put one foot in front of the other, to walk, you have to betray yourself. A moment that goes on all life long.

And truth? Where is truth? Is it always servicing deception? Or is it the violation itself? A violation that can't get undone, that you keep trying to undo. That you keep trying to fill with more violation. You keep trying to right a sense of betrayal as you grow with it.

When I was a teen I read the Song of Songs over and over. The sensuous love in it saved me. Love of God perhaps, but love. Skin love. And I thought of the sacrifices of fruit and wheat and animals, the scent of spices, the blood splattered on the altar. My heart goes up in smoke. I wish I could say, dissolved in the beloved. But my tears won't let me.

*   *   *

M.E.:   Better stop talking about things I don't know about. There's something eerie in the atmosphere. Poison in the air. I know about my work. My life and work. What else is there to share?

CHAPTER NINE

Faith and destructiveness

D r Michael Eigen was interviewed in September 2006 by the New York Institute for Psychotherapy Training by faculty member and supervisor, Dr Regina Monti.

RM: Throughout your writings, there is a thematic grounding of faith. In *The Sensitive Self* (2004), you describe the infant's agony and hunger for the mother (the Other) leading the infant into a "numbness, stupor, oblivion". When mother shows up, the infant is full with the "Bountiful Other . . . whose merciful intervention enables restoration of aliveness." You go on to say that "something of this pattern remains as an organizing sequence . . . informing emotional life". Disintegration–integration, fragmentation–wholeness, etc. Is this the arena of faith? A definition of faith?

Along with faith, you write often about destructiveness. So much destruction in the Bible (a book of Faith). Where does the therapist's faith originate in sitting and witnessing with the patient his/her trauma, destruction and shattering?

ME: I'd like to start by taking these first two questions together. The problem of faith and destructiveness is basic to the human condition. Many sessions I write about are felt to be crises of faith.

Faith in face of destructiveness. Can faith survive destruction? In what way? How?

As you know, a person sours in face of injury. Disillusionment can lead to cynicism, an embittered personality, an embittered soul. One hardens. We've learned that even fragmentation can harden. Diffusion can harden. Personality dispersal can become a chronic defence, a self-hardening. And if one touches it, one finds injury. A baby faith devastated. Often devastation one never recovers from, not fully.

We may give reasons why we use unnecessary violence, like wiping out Dresden, like Hiroshima and Nagasaki. Unnecessary violence. Like the Nazi concentration camps. Like so much wiping each other out on the global scene today. We point to politics, economics, national "self-interest". Why does so much professed self-interest have to be so destructive, including destructive to the "interest" it professes to advance? It may be jejune of me to say that one reason is our injured baby faith, soul injury that remains with us all life long, looking for expression, correction. We are caught in a dreadful law: injury leads to injury.

We get a thrill from acts of obliteration. The biblical God is a model of our psyche on this score. What's his response to feeling hurt by how badly his human creation turns out, human beings a blow to his ego? He wants to wipe the human race out, blot it out. With a flood. Throughout the Bible, one emotional flood or another tries to wipe out destructiveness. Destruction wiping out destruction. This primal response shows how prone we are to respond to difficulty and injury by trying to blot it out, obliterate it. Because we feel wiped out by it. Because we are partial beings who ache for total states.

A lot of therapy is about the slow recovery of faith, at least more of it, a more informed faith, wiser, fuller, ready for anything. Although we can never be so ready. A respectful faith. In which caring has a real place, a caring about one's destructiveness. To care enough to struggle with it.

In my twin books, *Toxic Nourishment* and *Damaged Bonds*, I describe how people are poisoned by what nourishes them, damaged by bonds that sustain them, that give them life. You mention a rhythm I describe in *The Sensitive Self*, a basic rhythm. Therapy supports or tries to jump-start a rhythm of coming through injury, defeat, megalomania, a rhythm one goes through over and over, a rhythm of faith.

RM: You have written that the post-Freudian interest and deeper exploration of psychotic process has allowed psychoanalysis to "come out of the closet". Please explain. What is the closet? Who and/or what is in there?

ME: Although Freud ostensibly developed a theory and clinical approach to neurosis, I point out in *The Psychotic Core* that his concepts are heavily steeped in a phenomenology of psychosis. The id: seething cauldron of emotional realities where the law of contradiction and common sense do not hold, where space and time are abrogated, compressed, nullified (and in some ways expanded). The superego: persecution gone haywire, spinning into self-hate, self-demolition, a mixture of self-torment and self-obliteration. The ego: at once a hallucinatory organ and adaptive agent with anti-hallucinogenic properties. Freud wrote that an early cognitive operation of the ego is hallucination. For example, the ego as wish-fulfilment machine, attempting to get rid of disturbance by making believe it's not there in some way, wishing it away. A problem with wishing disturbance away is one tends to wish oneself away as well. A vanishing tendency is initiated that becomes objectless or something like all-inclusive. In extremis, a vanishing tendency that vanishes itself as well as anything in its path.

Freud spoke of flooding as a primal trauma. And one way one deals with emotional storm is by trying to wish it, hallucinate it, out of existence. A problem being, one hallucinates oneself out of existence, too.

So, one thing I brought out is how psychotic states informed the background and construction of Freud's structural concepts, and that psychosis was crucial to his theory and practice from the outset.

As psychoanalysis unfolded, attention gravitated to psychotic states: Melanie Klein, Harry Stack Sullivan, Searles, Winnicott, Fairbairn, Bion. In 1975, Andre Green formalized this seismic shift in psychoanalysis in his statement that where once neurosis was a defence against perverse tendencies, now both were seen as ways of warding off and organizing psychotic anxieties. Henry Elkin, steeped in Jung and the British school, used to lecture, "Behind every neurosis is a hidden psychosis".

It seems to me after two world wars, the shift towards madness was inevitable. Although, of course, madness has never been a stranger to the human race. Now we can add pervasive psychopathy to the pie. For our own moment of history has, as a guiding light, the calculated, psychopathic manipulation of psychotic anxieties. We have just seen one of the great power grabs in our nation's history, certainly the most amazing in my seventy-odd years, a basic weapon being manipulation of catastrophic dreads. Bodies are paying for it and, I believe, the psychic health of nations.

RM: In your work, your refer to "states of consciousness." For example, you write: "We are challenged to work with cosmic and practical I-feelings". I love this statement. Would you explain further?

ME: In many of my books I write about the challenge of being in multiple worlds at once. Pluralistic dimensions of experience. One might speak of tendencies, capacities, attitudes. Different worlds open with different modes of approach. For example, when immersed in taste, touch, vision, hearing, worlds open in each that the others can't offer.

With this in mind, one appreciates the implicit humour in Bion's references to "common sense". How to co-ordinate the senses is no small wonder. In autism, for example, attention is pulled first by something pre-eminent in one sense, then another. So that common sense, the senses working together, becomes quite a challenge, a genuine achievement.

And yet each sense gives us inexhaustible worlds, gives us ourselves differently. There is no end to the nuances of self-feeling, the self-sensations that our senses modulate, ineffable pathways. Yes, sensation is ineffable.

How much more so is the challenge, the invitation, to get to know, to taste, to smell different worlds along the cosmic–personal dimension. In *The Psychotic Core* I showed intricacies of being both anonymous and personal beings. We are made up of many anonymous capacities that work by themselves and we sense this anonymity that pervades our existence. Yet, we have personal feeling, personal self-feeling, I, me, you, we. A feeling of my personal being. Winnicott, for example, is exercised by the question of how personal self-feeling extends to embrace and grapple with anonymous processes that make it up.

It may be that Federn was the first to write about this systemati-
cally. He, following Freud, felt that the I, at first, is a kind of cosmic
I, boundless, no end to surface or depth, if these spatial terms apply
at all. Psychotic individuals he worked with failed to make the tran-
sition to it into their body envelope. They refused or were unable to
squeeze into the limiting field of usual material and social reality.
The ability to contract the cosmic I-feeling to fit a common sense
world did not undergo sufficient development. I won't cover all this
ground again here. Just using this to note the difficulty the demand
of living in and co-ordinating different regions of being can bring.
Part of therapy involves a certain double (multiple) directionality:
worlds open with movement of sensation fields and worlds narrow
and close. The rhythm of opening–closing, expanding–narrowing is
part of basic rhythms that need to evolve. Therapy tries to support
evolution of capacities to nourish each other.

Mystics also attest to impalpable, ineffable awareness. This is a
very real capacity that stamps experience. It plays an important role
in creativity, personal transformation and deformation, and also
horrendous individual and group scenarios. For we squeeze a sense
of the infinite into time–space scripts that can be uplifting, or
murderous, or both. Note the fusion of infinite satisfactions in
suicide bombing, where devotion and obliteration merge, an
approach to a totalistic experience that is hard to match in ability to
satisfy competing strivings.

How to confess we are at a loss what to do with ourselves, with
all we are and have been given, with all we can do?! We are like
babies who have not yet developed frames of reference that do
justice to experience, this sense of being, streams not only of sensations, but infinities of worlds within and without. I am glad you
love the sentence you ask me about. It shows a love of the mystery
we are part of.

RM: I am confused by the discussion in your book, *Damaged
Bonds*, regarding the idea that with traumatized, or what Bion refers
to as "shattered", patients, the analyst needs to "dream the patient".
"Dream" in the sense of imagine? Or literally dream as in during
sleep? Or both?

ME: Bion remarks in *Cogitations* (1992), "I am his other self and it
is a dream". You let this resonate, let it seep in. Sometimes I play

with a resonant statement like this: I am his other. I am his dream. I am his other dream. We are indeed each other's selves, each other's dreams.

In *Cogitations*, Bion develops the notion that dreaming is part of our psychic digestive system. In *Damaged Bonds* and other places, I rework this somewhat and put it this way. Dreams, in part, help initiate digestion of catastrophic impacts. They help feed trauma globs into the stream of experience and try to begin the processing of injury. Often we don't know what wounds us or the extent of the wound. It hits, and if there are enough hits or big enough hits, we are in danger of going under. We deform to work with unbearable impacts. There is always more than we can ever possibly digest. But we try to break off, bite off some bit of trauma glob or chunk and chew on it, turn it this way and that, dream it, rework it, develop expressive symbols and gestures. In some form or other, through dance, music, painting, poetry, hopefully psychotherapy, we slowly develop, over thousands of years, an emotional language, a digestive language.

Politics, economics, public affairs potentially does this, too. With modern technology the stakes are greater, nearly instantaneously global. And if the digestive process goes wrong—and often it does—we are left with global representations of trauma that escalate the trauma chain, increase the trauma momentum. The digestive system is broken.

Bion calls attention to the deep fact that our emotional digestive system can be damaged, our psychic digestive system damaged, dream-work damaged, primary process damaged. The impact of massive trauma is through and through. It is not a matter, as in the old model, of secondary process working on primary process. The new model is that primary process itself plays an important role in the digestion of affects. And if primary process is warped and damaged, no amount of secondary process "correction" will correct this. We will add warp upon warp and make the whole in some way even more monstrous. It would be a macabre caricature to say we are in danger of chronic psychic indigestion. The situation is much worse. People are paying for this damaged capacity with their lives.

That is why, in *Psychic Deadness*, in a chapter titled "Primary process and shock", I call the analyst an auxiliary dream processor, rather than auxiliary ego. For primary process needs long-term support. And this support partly comes by profound self-to-self interweaving, unconscious permeability, in which we taste each other's self-substance, a kind of mutual steeping. It is a process that is needed in cultural as well as personal dreamwork.

RM: You (like Winnicott, Bion, and Lacan) have found a personal language, a unique voice in psychoanalysis and methodology. Your idiosyncratic use of language, the experience-near aspect of reading your work manifests, I feel, from the ability to blend the deeply personal with the historical–theoretical. Your work is at times unabashedly autobiographical, experiential, and self-revealing. In light of the issue of self-disclosure in psychoanalytic work, please comment on the evolution and use of your personal experience in your analytic work.

You often cluster your thoughts/observations/case studies around specific human emotions/feelings: e.g., *Lust*, *Rage*, *Ecstasy*. Why these particular emotions, and how has this methodology served to express your professional experiences/observations?

ME: Thanks, Regina, for these thoughts. Let me try putting these two questions together. When I wrote *Ecstasy*, my intent was to give expression to something that made my life worthwhile, something at the very heart of my experience. An ecstatic core at the heart of life. Yet, when I got into it and tried to let come out what wanted to speak, I found myself gravitating more and more to destructive ecstasies. For there is something about ecstatic destruction that is world threatening at this moment of history. Destruction of the conditions that support life, the atmosphere, the water, the air. The hole in the ozone layer parallels a hole in our own selves through which toxins spill, emotional toxins, affective attitudes that damage rather than support existence. This is happening on a wide scale with accelerating momentum. But there must be something we can do.

When I speak about damaged primary process and dreamwork, I am speaking about damaged processes that support emotional life, that support psychic life, that support us. We breathe each other as feeling beings, breathe in feelings and attitudes and expel them, too. We live in a psychic atmosphere that is very sensitive. We have sensitivity that can evolve to support our psychic atmosphere and enable it to support us. But we seem to be heading in another direction and getting a kick out of doing so.

Our current bully government seems to get well nigh ecstatic from the exercise of power, even though they are like drunk elephants in the china shop of the world. They know what they are doing. They know how to make fortunes and create power for themselves and their corporate base. But they do not seem to care about the damage their *jouissance* causes. A kind of psychopathic element rules the day. But it is not the only element. It is now the only path we can take. So many of us want something better, fuller, more caring than this. A caring for the conditions that support life. A caring for the emotional conditions which support us. A caring for our human health, which is falling behind the pace of spiritual toxic spills.

The second book in this series, *Rage,* caught a ruling feeling of the time. Every day news reports spoke of one kind of rage or another, race rage, terrorist rage, road rage, computer rage, alcoholic–addictive rage, you name it. Rage appeared to be a core affect in our nation and I tried to put some tracers on it. I tried to turn the experience of rage around, something like a kaleidoscope, and touch it in many contexts from many angles. Through art, literature, religion, clinical sessions, politics. I used anything I could, anything that was part of me, that could let rage speak and dig into and open our rage world. There is, for example, a smouldering rage against the inflated power egos that flaunt dumbfounding success while multitudes look on and cringe. Great Macy parade balloon egos inflated with and feeding on the resentment of many, playing with fire.

The last book in this series, *Lust,* came out just this year. My own experiences of lust, ecstasy, and rage play an important role in these works. But lust, too, took me deeper into the body politic and the lust for power. It straddles individual and group activities. A particular lust dear to me, writing lust, poetry lust, received some care and poets will, I think, like what I say about their particular addiction, what poetry opens.

Tradition tells us death haunts lust and this notion is no stranger to psychoanalysis. I use some of Lacan's writings on death in lust to heighten the interplay of our pairing of lust and mortality. A premature dying haunts experience, as if we drag a kind of self-deadening process like a weight. Self-deadening we try to deny. Again, I fear, if we don't find ways to face this coupling of heightened aliveness–self deadening, we will create overly destructive mimicry of these states. We are doing so with alarming consistency in public affairs, where sensitivity to human feeling is for losers.

My latest book, *Feeling Matters*, should be out any month, any day. It builds on these themes and pleads for the importance of feeling in personal life and in public life. It shows how insensitivity spirals, wreaking havoc on a national and global scale. In one chapter, for example, "Election rape", I trace the resonance between a case of child abuse and this same person as an adult feeling raped by the 2000 presidential election and much that followed. She was sensitized to rape in daily life, and felt it keenly in the body politic as well as in her own body. A confluence between childhood trauma and adult trauma opened reality in important ways.

While this new book is concerned with fits between personal and group trauma, it also opens domains beyond trauma and appeals to an ethics of sensitivity with psycho-spiritual roots. This work explores ways that faith meets catastrophic impacts and helps support the beginning of processing them, ways of working with them. An affirmation of life in the midst of horror. We have much work to do.

Thank you, Regina, for your questions, your care, your exuberant sensitivity.

Author's note

There is a lot wrong. Not just a matter of princess and pea or sand in oyster. The irritant runs through us. Perhaps it is life itself. An intrinsic part of life.

There are myths and stories about The Irritant as far back as writing takes us. Some are organized around something lost or missing. A body cut in half, a soul cut in half, halves seeking each other. There is psychoanalytic writing about placenta as the lost part (Eigen, 2006a; Lacan, 1978; Rhode, 1994) One writer (Tustin, 1995) imagines a tearing apart of the tongue and nipple, although she also writes of a universal broken heart. Early psychoanalysts wrote a lot about loss of womb or breast. Gnostics envisioned the soul losing heaven as it descends into womb, birth, earth. For many mystics, the soul's separation from God felt like the primary rift, or gap, or rupture. The list can be multiplied to include economic and social alienation and, on a more personal plane, rupture between true and false self.

Separation and loss is one pole, something violent, explosive, or impinging another. Not that separation or loss is not violent. But there is eruption as well as rupture. Attack from the outside is an obvious instance. So many dreams depict assault, body or house broken into. Literal dangers, yes, but also expressions of psyche broken into. A sense of violation perforating physical and psychic integrity.

Not simply psyche broken into, but also broken. There are age-old references to corruption of soul or spirit, something rotten or ill, a worm or canker in the rose. For St Augustine, God was, among other things, the Physician.

In our day, reference to self, or soul, or personality does not simply involve a flaw (hubris, sin, corruption). It has blossomed into a language of fragmentation. Alienation, entropy, meaning-lessness, emptiness, nothingness. Also pulverization, bits and pieces, splitting, falling apart. From a language of neurosis to a language of psychosis. From perpetual crises to perpetual break-down. Mythic tropes of catastrophe have become personalized and socialized. What is forever at stake is some form of psychic annihilation.

Something off or wrong or annihilating may come from within or without. There are many variations. One psychoanalytic scenario involves a doubleness inherent in excitement. A sexual or aggressive surge, for example, may be at once pleasurable and threatening. In certain instances, it can be disorganizing, even to the point of shatter. A perennial tug of war between arousal and control can give way to collapse and dispersal. It is also possible to harden oneself and use sex and aggression for narrow ends. Collapse and self-hardening are not mutually exclusive.

It may be, as Bion (1970) points out, that the advent of psychic life is itself catastrophic or has catastrophic elements. It also seems to be the case that something beatific runs through it. There are instances in which even the most cruel destructiveness carries ecstatic components, e.g., orgasmic aspects of rage (Eigen, 2002).

Images of aggression have mushroomed to apocalyptic proportions. There are still great disasters of nature that trigger apocalyptic images. But the horror of our weaponry has added new fuel to annihilation anxieties. Can you imagine a leader of our country taking public pleasure, even self-satisfaction, in an anticipated "shock and awe" of the bombing of a foreign city? Owing to public media, a psychic gorilla pounding his breast takes the chilling thrill of what used to be called "barbarous" or "animal" behaviour to new heights in the murder of a segment of a human population. This is a tenor of the times now, not two hundred or two thousand years ago. Human beings at this moment treating each other in blood-curdling ways in not a few places throughout the world. Images of this maltreatment blown up on the screens of our minds through nearly instantaneous media transmission. And yet, it continues here and elsewhere.

Another piece of something wrong is the inordinate reliance of public leaders on deception, on winning lies (Eigen, 1996). Political constellations or amalgams of religious fundamentalists and corporate interests mediated by government leaders are taking a great human toll. Theocratic and financial mania threaten the viability and goodness of life. What is at stake is not only physical life, but quality of psychical life. Theocratic and financial interests seem to have little qualms about gobbling up or getting rid of whatever stands in their way. It is not clear what is being exported when we say we are exporting democracy, but whatever it is looks ugly indeed.

All this to say we cannot get away from ourselves. Wherever we are, something wrong happens. It is the way we are made and the way life is constituted. Not only because we feel the impacts of things that do not jibe with our needs as wrong, but because we are beset with needs, desires, imaginings that make trouble for ourselves and others. Processes that constitute us make us problematic to ourselves.

We live in a violent universe, yet conceive wishes for a non-violent life. We live in a predator–prey life zone, life feeds on life, yet are touched by a vision of basic kindness. Our generalizing mind conceives of kindness for all. It is part of our vision that every person is precious, yet we take pleasure in inflicting terror.

A long way to go. We do not know whether a vision of helping one another is feasible or how far it can reach. Some of us will not and cannot settle for less. Perhaps that means not being able to settle for less than the impossible, the impossibly good, rather than all too possible shock and horror.

The something wrong, then, is not just in our political and economic systems, limned as they are with militaristic ardour. Our systems reflect us. We make them. The something wrong is us, or part of us: we are what is wrong. We are our greatest challenge.

Today, this something wrong takes the form of pervasive, ominous destructiveness. But what it is, how it is made, who we are, and what we become are open questions, nodal points of evolution.

Something wrong: Grace

The following version of "Something wrong" was written by invitation for the woman's online journal, *Moondance* (June–September 2006; www.moondance.org/.webloc). It is a one-woman play in which Grace's lines are extracted and reworked from the longer original in Chapter Seven. Martha Frisoli Gibson supplied stage directions.

Something Wrong: Grace

A darkened stage, lit only by a bulb above the figure of a pensive woman, Grace, who is seated on a stool.

It's not just that they make you feel wrong, but that you *are* The Wrong. An avatar of The Wrong. As far back as I remember I was The Wrong. And part of the feeling is the sense that I am Their Wrong. Wrong for them, wrong for everyone. As a little girl, I searched for someone who didn't see me as The Wrong, someone for whom I mattered. I almost found it in teachers, but not quite.

My hospitalizations started in my teens. Maybe in hospitals the good would happen. If it did, it did not get through to me. I was an uncorrectable imprint of The Wrong. And I saw The Wrong in grown-ups who were trying to help me. I had a sick sense that even helpers made me a special conduit of the wrong they breathed, a taint no one could bear. The Wrong swallowed up the world.

Inquisitors torture you into realizing you are The Wrong, then leave you. They stick The Wrong into you and do not need you until the next surge. The Wrong is like a sex urge in them that builds, climaxes, then leaves for awhile. When it builds, they need me to put it into.

Underneath a face is another face, a knife that lives in blood and pain. A famished knife. Does it take a psychotic to see insides of humans as hungry knives?

I turned to Jesus with total intensity when I was a little girl. Someone who got it - who knew The Wrong, the pain, and triumphed over it. Jesus, a lightning rod for The Wrong of this world.

My mind is a mist. Was Jesus the more of life? Did he triumph over life? A greater life? The fall back to myself was always hard. Back on earth there was just me. Jesus did not clean The Wrong out of me. I was still unclean me. The Wrong is part of my essence, part of the pulse of life.

There are moments of joy in which one transcends The Wrong. The Wrong is eclipsed by joy. One appreciates such moments but The Wrong comes back with a wallop.

I hear the words of the psalm, *"I am poor and destitute, my heart has died within me."* This feels like something right. It is not that I am dead when I feel these words. No, it's as if The Wrong dies while these words live. As if The Wrong is the cross of this world and there are, for moments, saving words. Soul words that live, a kind of life that cancels The Wrong. While I am alive in these words The Wrong does not win. One is a trauma I will never recover from. The other, a death that passes into life.

Grace rises and begins to slowly crisscross the area close to her stool.

Was there ever a time before Something Wrong? I don't think so. There was something wrong in the Garden of Eden! A snake telling lies, tempting stories with links to destruction. Our lives are stories, God's stories, I used to think. I still feel God very close to us, closer than ever. Sometimes I am ashamed for not hating God more.

We are the garden, the liars, the story telling snakes. The sea, the air, the animals, the flowers compacted in us. We are destructive creativity. As God is.

Garden of Eden, garden of evil. Some people really lie and pass real lies off as truth. Like making up a God story and saying it really happened when it is really a literary event, a spiritual event. We tell stories about a destructive urge in the garden of life. Are we afraid to say that we like this destructive urge? That this urge is a way into life?

Is this secret? The garden gives birth to destruction, is destructive birthing, nourishes destruction. Inside the nursing infant and caring mother, do I see snakes? When does belief becomes destructive? Is it madness of religions, to imagine destruction-free life as they destroy?

Grace peers out at the audience intently.

We imagine being expelled from the Garden because we need to imagine a place that is destruction free. A place to look back at or forward to. We look away from the fact that destruction was already in the garden, waiting for us as part of us.

The garden tells us it feels good to be alive. Yet, destruction comes. We are appalled at the need to destroy and draw back and double in on ourselves, and try to think beyond destruction, think of ways to outwit destruction. Ways to use destruction to some day return to a destruction-free place, or create one. A place we can only imagine.

And, what is real? Making believe destruction doesn't exist? Pretending to be masters of destruction? Hiding? Doing what we can?

Grace pauses. An expectant look encompasses her face.
Then she settles back against the stool, half-on, half-off.

The Wrong . . . The Wrong in Itself . . . a Kantian, Platonic Wrong. Such is my essence, mirrored back to me in the news:

A girl killed by her stepfather. A picture of her, tied in a chair, eating dog food, beaten, starved, thin as a feather. The usual uproar, investigation, jailing. A story falls into the newspaper about her mother in jail, weeping, saying she's a good mother. Each day the paper adds another story, then, it vanishes.

Did the mother and her husband try to kill The Wrong? It is a knot: people try to kill The Wrong, but The Wrong kills people. To say I see myself as that girl would be an injustice to her death. *But she is in me.* I am a lucky her, alive in this room with you, with your Wrong, our Wrongs together. We are lucky because we leave each other after only minutes together.

Time protects us.

Let us tolerate being Wrong together.

Grace smiles.

Wrong meets Wrong.

We survive this meeting.

In so much real life such a meeting blows up, crashes, even leads to death. Wrong against Wrong, an excuse to kill. War takes over and sweeps people along. What led to this girl's murder, what swept them along? It takes less than forty-five minutes to kill someone, but with her it built up over months.

A story said she was rambunctious: instead of giving in to her stepfather's shaming - like *I* did to *my* parents - she got worse, troublesome, obnoxious.

And he killed her.

She died rather than give in. I gave in, and became crazy. And am here with you today.

Devil inflamed devil. A little girl's cheeky energy inflamed tyranny. We are attacked and attack back, whether or not attacks are rightly aimed. The energy of a little girl mutilates a maimed adult. Not exactly a mini-mirror of aggression-to-aggression on the world stage, but not totally removed from it, either. Personalities wronging each other, without resources to meet The Wrong.

Do we *really* survive each other? I said we do. But I spoke too fast. We survive partly. It's not survival here, but change. Something happens for the worse. If we go far enough into the worse, we change. Wrong never goes away, but something happens when we grip it. I go into your Wrong, you into mine. I find mine through yours, you through mine. To touch the worse. Most people most of the time try to get *out* of it when the job is to get *into* it.

Freedom is working with The Wrong. I feel free when I don't have to make believe I'm right.

Grace pauses, clearly to replenish her self. When she continues, it is with refreshment, with renewed ability to deliver her wisdom.

My parents made believe they were right, and I made believe with them.

I have a paralysed brain.

When I was little, I had so many scary dreams—murderers, spiders, witches, devils. One I had over and over: shit everywhere. Everyone was angry and I was ashamed. They wanted things to be clean. I was like the girl the stepfather killed, messing things, spoiling things. Now I see a grown-up world with shit everywhere, wars, deaths, spoiling the world we live in. It's not just me. The feeling it's just you is so deep, but it's us, we're doing it, our shitty selves, our shitty psyches. It's as if my childhood dreams are being dreamt and lived by everyone.

Grace sighs . . . ponders . . . then brightens.

I went to a lovely restaurant last night! The first course was so good. Then the waitress vanished. The service ended. We waited and waited. I was having a good time so I didn't notice the main dish was taking too long. Should I make a fuss, express a grievance, or wait it out? I didn't want to create a disturbance and spoil a nice evening.

Then I thought, asking what happened to the food wouldn't be creating a disturbance. It's just a question, a reminder. I got more and more annoyed, afraid to ask. I was on the verge of ruining a good evening by not saying anything or saying too much. Couldn't I just say, "How's the food coming?"

Even if I pressed them and said something sarcastic like, "Forget about us?" or "What happened to the food?" or "Something wrong?" it wouldn't be the end of the world.

But inside, I felt it would be—it would be the end of the world. How to preserve the overall good feeling yet express a grievance became a major problem.

Not being able to solve the problem of whether to speak or not or how reminds me of a night I came out of one of my hospitalizations and stood by a street lamp on a corner, suddenly seized by grief over humanity, the whole human race. I was weeping, and people looked fearful and concerned. I must have given off "stay away" vibes, because no one came close to help me.

I saw Humanity and The Ages pass before my eyes. The grief of humankind from its beginning, all the pain of life, all time condensed in a moment of agony. I cried and cried yet felt very good, deep in contact with myself. I felt in contact with deep truth, deep life.

When it subsided, I realized there was a vast distance between what it feels like inside, and the outside world. A chasm that could grow and grow. I had an inkling that if I went all the way inside I'd be back in the hospital. It hit me that all the contact with your inside world won't necessarily enable you to make contact with the outside world. You could as easily go farther and farther away, with people and things seeming less and less real. I haven't gone that far. I feel life is real even when I feel it is not. I don't think I could reach a point where nothing is real, but you never know.

I need to find a way to keep the inside contact I have, to further it, yet link up with life outside me. It may take my whole life to do it, or do it well, if well is possible.

I got fooled by the feeling of newness. I used to think *feeling* new meant *being* new. Now I know the trap of thinking you are a new person. You think you are transformed but that is not you. You think: *This is IT.*

But it fades, and you are you. You are you with maybe a little more IT.

I cried and cried when I realized I'd have to lose my new beginning. Then I thought, well, you don't exactly lose it. It's that you're not so fooled by it. It can be there, part of the mix, but not a pretend substitute for the whole mix.

Instead you say, "Well, here I am. Here I am." And where does that leave me?

I'm me, looking at you.

Not bad, huh?

With a huge, somewhat smiling yawn, Grace stretches.

Damage triggers attempts at recovery. Brain tissues try to recover after stroke or seizure. Maybe they try to recover after medication.

But what if medication never stops? You can't tell the difference between healing and damage.

When I was in the hospital I feared my brain was disintegrating. Was that medication, or disease? Disease, I think. Dread of disintegrating was part of my breakdown. I was disintegrating. Sometimes it concentrated in my head, my brain. It spread all over. It was me myself disintegrating. I told a doctor, "If only you could tell me my brain isn't really disintegrating, I could get through this."

At one point they tried electric shock and I blacked out. When I came to, I disintegrated. I literally saw the world in pieces, an awkward collage, my I a mosaic of tiles that didn't fit. They stopped after two or three tries. Thank God they recognized it made me worse.

I don't mind going through what I need to go through as long as I know it is me, and not my brain, that is disintegrating. If it is me, I can go on.

I will let you in on something secret: my body is a war zone. Intense combat goes on. Missiles streak across my organs, making my skin break out in rashes. Maggots in my blood wait for a chance to eat through veins. I'm filled with tumours. I've had three face-lifts today and already I'm sagging. I'm going to have liposuction. Or is it another kind of suction I want, sucking my psyche and making it better, making it go away.

All is luminous. Light, Light, Light. But it does not make the maggots go away.

Today, I woke determined to go through Everything! Nothing would stop me! The attack came and I dropped into it, whirled. *Today is the day I will go all the way.* I will not end the agony with no end. *This time,* I will see what happens. I will go with it forever until something happens. And if nothing happens, I will not stop. *I must find out.* I must see what It is made of. What I'm made of. This is IT.

No matter how hard I tried, It began to ebb and I rose above It, watching, wondering how this happened. It was familiar, being above. Something I take for granted. I probably do not realize it is happening most of the time. But this time I felt the difference, the contrast, being in It and above It. It's me both ways, double me. Single me as double me, double me in single me. Is that where the idea of Trinity comes from, one as three, three as one? Me being aware of me being aware of me?

I became very tired. You know, I've been tired all my life—psychically anaemic. Not enough soul oxygen. Not enough O, or too much O. Asleep with one part of me, and awake with one part of me, active and fatigued at the same time.

You dive in, and there is no end. There is no air. You squint and start to die, and panic. It's like looking into a crystal ball and seeing war. You'd think I'd be happy but I'm humiliated. I mainly feel humiliation. I am not up to being me. I am not up to the job I set for myself, a total birth, a going through, a sticking with. I fall asleep on myself and it's all over. There's no chance of It happening again today. Maybe tomorrow . . .

A long, deliberate pause. Grace settles on to the stool.

My meditator says, "Go back to a safe place." But there is no safe place. There was no safe place in my house, no safe place for feeling.

My meditator says, "Find someone to comfort you." She means a comforting presence within, a residue from childhood. "Picture someone who comforted you. Feel the comfort."

"Are you kidding?!" I break down in inconsolable fury and grief. Did she say, did I imagine it, "Don't go back to crying." She *did* say it.

She was worried. Or disgusted or frustrated, impatient at my being stuck so long. All my life there is this hole in the ice and when I fall in—and I do fall in, often—there is danger of a chill that will never go away. Ice on the outside, chill on the inside. Thermo- what do you call it? Thermo—something bad.

I hate my outside chill, stiff skin, tight face. I don't think many people really like the way I look. I don't think I make many people feel comfortable. I think some appreciate a certain nervous intensity. They sense I'm in contact with something, that I have something to offer, something mad perhaps. Something to offer, a little like a poet might. Some thought or word from somewhere else.

I see people watching me dig into myself, through myself, through the ice, deep under. To say I might drown misses the point. I am drowned. I'm a drowned person. I speak from under the ice, within the thermocline.

Do you know what a thermocline is? That's the word—thermocline. It's a deep chill. A chill that once was feeling. Horror perhaps, sorrow, despair, giving up, never giving up, fighting in the freeze, through the freeze, with the freeze. Is this the angel Jacob wrestled with—or did he have a warm one? My angel is a thermocline. I wrestle with my thermocline.

If I go back, like my meditator urges, it's to shutdown. I tell her there's no place to go back to that's worth going to.

She says, "Then let yourself be comforted as if you had been." She imagines you can imagine comfort even if you've never had it. She takes comfort for granted.

To hell with her. Let her be alarmed, irritated! Niceness is not nice enough. I smell vanity. She is hurt that she can not be a comforting presence for me, that there is someone she can not comfort. Failure of a human or spiritual power she thinks she has, wants to have, she has for many, but not for me. With me she is still a spiritual wannabe. I torture her by being an exception. She can't endure the torture scent that comes from me. The torture that is me may not be something she can know. She may be too well meaning.

I come to the end of her personality and she of mine, and I break down and sob.

It's too much!

Still seated, Grace nervously taps her right foot.

A void is at the core of my personality, perhaps is the core. Under all the activity, the flux, the business—void. I've covered it with hysteria, thinking, doing. I've been fighting it all my life. Void scared me.

Though I'm getting less scared of it. It's a relief to give in to its fascination, its pleasures. I thought giving in meant I would have to accept defeat. To feel it there without thrashing, to accept something would always be missing, that part of me would be missing. I had no idea how tingly being void can be.

It's not just emptiness. It's more like I'm not there. And not being there is a relief, a joy.

Anxiety is another core. There's an alphabet of the soul, a psychic alphabet, a core alphabet. Void is one core, anxiety another. It's not that anxiety fills the void. It can try but doesn't succeed. The void continues beneath it, beyond it. Anxiety is a void of its own, a world of its own, a background nearly always there, ready to overwhelm. The void sometimes swallows it, tries to dampen it, shut it down. There are times when the void and anxiety fight to be Number 1. They fight for the same space. At the same time, each creates space of its own. They are antagonists, but also go their own ways, not bothering with each other.

I used to attribute each to my parents—their anxiety, their emptiness. Flooding me with anxiety, leaving me empty. I'd fight and give in, lost and angry. Scared of anxiety. I'd fight it off, shut it out, as if it shouldn't be there, like a bug trying to thrash its way out of molasses. To open to anxiety. Is that possible? To open instead of fighting, open as well as fight. It's bigger than parents, more than me. Void and anxiety—a, b, c.

My mind is chilled, frozen. It was easier in school. You read what you had to and found what you needed. My mind got knocked out by my marriage. Sexual madness followed. Relationships broke me as a person. I kept thinking something good was happening and then the freeze came. Something more than rejection or failure. Something broke me apart. The good in the universe became a broken thing and I tried to hold my broken insides together. The world looked like broken insides. Wherever I moved, wherever I looked, I was living in a world of broken insides.

I remember the moment when reading became different. I felt the author's presence, near me, inside me. His insides in my insides. The first time it happened I got scared and put the book down. But I knew something important happened, something healing. It was a great moment when I realized that books were filled with people's insides and that their insides fed mine. A kind of miracle, to need an invisible presence, to want someone who is not there, who may have died long ago, whose words touch me.

There is music in the writing. It's not simply in the words. It comes from what is full in another person. It comes from another's void. When I feel that, my void is at peace.

I'm touching a secret place I'd go to get away from my parents. It was a safe place then, but not *always* safe. Panic would flood it like a broken dam rushing over an old, dry riverbed. Cores meld. Now this secret place feels like my deepest truth.

There are outer and inner shells. My personality is an outer shell. It hovers with this interest, that hope, no peace in it. Peace is in the void. The void is big true, hysterical me is little true. Oscillating trues give birth to lots of trues.

Grace shifts, crosses one knee then re-crosses with the other. Her breath quickens, eyes light. As if entering a trance, she rises.

Last night I dreamt of a tiny baby. It is very tiny. I hold it. It is mine. It makes me more secure, related, comfortable, fuller, whole. I think all things are made of chaos and a baby comes of it. Tiny may be all I can handle. But now I do have that—for this dream moment. A moment I didn't have the moment before.

A baby survives the thermocline.

I think I'm saying that a birth is greater than death.

For everything starts off alive. Everything *is* alive. Womb thoughts. Dream as part of womb activity. Dream wombs.

Dreams are like a respirator in an intensive care ward inside us. They help keep life alive. An umbilicus to the World Soul.

To give birth to a dream! Or is it the other way—dreams give birth to us? Dreams as birthing activity. Is the I something dreaming births?

We dip into dreams to taste our lives raw, a sense that in dreams we are naked, that dreams touch truth about our basic selves.

Dreams keep psychic life alive. Like a baby, they take hits, go under, get damaged. Mutilated dreams, dreams of mutilation—glimpses of our damaged selves. They keep coming, damage and all, deep monsters, moments of grace.

It's raining dreams! And when I look closely, every raindrop is a damaged baby and inside the baby is a damaged dream and inside the dream a damaged baby.

Yet damage doesn't stop us! Dreams are partly crippled bodies that say, "Throw away your crutches and fly!" I'm above the rooftops, high. You can't stop where dreams come from. You can't escape seeing how gnarled you are. You don't outgrow being a damaged baby. You just grow.

And my womb, the limitless ever-forming Void? The Great Void nothing can fill, pregnant emptiness?

Freud speaks of a dream navel with tangled root systems vanishing from view. The great umbilicus. Where does it lead? Unborn places, thoughts and feelings waiting for a chance at living.

Everything one feels changes the void. Everything a baby feels changes the void.

God says: *You will give birth in pain*. I take it, psychic birth. And joy is painful too? Yes, joy is painful. But joy is joyful.

Yes, joy is joyful.

REFERENCES

Balint, M. (1968). *The Basic Fault.* London: Routledge, 1979.

Bion, W. R. (1965). *Transformations.* London: Heinemann.

Bion, W. R. (1970). *Attention and Interpretation.* New York: Rowman & Littlefield, 1995.

Bion, W. R. (2005). *The Italian Seminars.* London: Karnac.

Brenner, W. H. (2001). Creation, causality and freedom of the will. In: R. L. Arrington & M. Addis (Eds.), *Wittgenstein and Philosophy of Religion.* London: Routledge.

Eigen, M. (1986). *The Psychotic Core.* London: Karnac, 2004.

Eigen, M. (1992). *Coming Through the Whirlwind.* Wilmette, IL: Chiron.

Eigen, M. (1995). *Reshaping the Self.* Madison, CT: Psychosocial Press (International Universities Press).

Eigen, M. (1996). *Psychic Deadness.* London: Karnac, 2004.

Eigen, M. (1999). *Toxic Nourishment.* London: Karnac.

Eigen, M. (2001a). *Ecstasy.* Middletown, CT: Wesleyan University Press.

Eigen, M. (2001b). *Rage.* Middletown, CT: Wesleyan University Press.

Eigen, M. (2002). *Rage.* Middletown, CT: Wesleyan University Press.

Eigen, M. (2004). *The Sensitive Self.* Middletown, CT: Wesleyan University Press.

Eigen, M. (2005). *Emotional Storm.* Middletown, CT: Wesleyan University Press.

Eigen, M. (2006a). *Lust*. Middletown, CT: Wesleyan University Press.

Eigen, M. (2006b). *Feeling Matters: From the Yosemite God to the Annihilated Self*. London: Karnac.

Eigen, M. (2007). *Age of Psychopathy*. Available online at http://www.psychoanalysis-and-therapy.com/human_nature/eigen/pref.html

Freud, S. (1937c). Analysis terminable and interminable. *S.E.*, *23*: 211–253. London: Hogarth.

Klein, M. (1946). Notes on some schizoid mechanisms. In: M. Klein, P. Heimann, S. Isaacs, & J. Riviere (Eds.), *Developments in Psycho-Analysis* (pp. 292–320). London: Hogarth, 1952.

Lacan, J. (1978). *The Four Fundamental Concepts of Psycho-Analysis*. J.-A. Miller (Ed.), A. Sheridan (Trans.). New York: Norton.

Lacan, J. (1993). *The Seminars of Jacques Lacan: Book III The Psychoses 1955–1956*. J.-A. Miller & R. R. Grigg (Eds.). New York: Norton.

Mowrer, O. H. (1964). *The New Group Therapy*. Princeton, NJ: D. Van Nostrand.

Rhode, E. (1994). *Psychotic Metaphysics*. London: Karnac.

Tustin, F. (1995). *Autism and Childhood Psychosis*. London: Karnac.

Winnicott, D. W. (1988). *Human Nature*. London: Free Association.

Wittgenstein, L. (1984). *Culture and Value*. G. H. von Wright (Ed.) in collaboration with H. Nyman, P. Winch (Trans). Chicago, IL: University of Chicago Press.

INDEX